87 PRACTICAL TIPS
FOR DYNAMIC SELLING

Phil

Lang mae yer lumb reek!!

For a complete list of Management Books 2000 titles,
visit our website on http://www.mb2000.com

87 PRACTICAL TIPS FOR DYNAMIC SELLING

*87 Practical tips <u>Guaranteed</u>
to increase your sales and profit*

*No holds barred!
A complete 'How To' guide*

David Yule

Copyright © David Yule 2005

All rights reserved. No part of this publication may be reproduced, stored in a retrieval system, or transmitted in any form or by any means, electronic, mechanical, photocopying, recording, or otherwise without the prior permission of the publishers.

First published in 2005 by Management Books 2000 Ltd
Reprinted in 2006 by Management Books 2000 Ltd
Forge House, Limes Road
Kemble, Cirencester
Gloucestershire, GL7 6AD, UK
Tel: 0044 (0) 1285 771441
Fax: 0044 (0) 1285 771055
E-mail: info@mb2000.com
Web: www.mb2000.com

Printed and bound in Great Britain by 4edge Ltd of Hockley, Essex - www.4edge.com

This book is sold subject to the condition that it shall not, by way of trade or otherwise, be lent, resold, hired out, or otherwise circulated without the publisher's prior consent in any form of binding or cover other than that in which it is published and without a similar condition including this condition being imposed upon the subsequent purchaser.

British Library Cataloguing in Publication Data is available
ISBN 1-85252-478-2

The Tips

Most salespeople know <u>what</u> they want to do		**9**
Introduction		**11**
1	You Can't Fail	15
2	Find Your Selling Style (and use it!)	16
3	Confirmation Bias	21
4	Cold Calling Techniques that Really Work	30
5	Word Power	32
6	Know When to Avoid the Most Dangerous Word in Selling	34
7	Know When to Use the Most Powerful Word in Selling	36
8	Use the Second Most Powerful Word in Selling	38
9	Problem v Concern	40
10	Coach v Help	42
11	Think	44
12	Sell What Is Personally Important	45
13	Acknowledge People	54
14	Make Positive Assumptions	56
15	Approach at the Right Time	57
16	Approach in the Right Way	58
17	Overviews	61
18	Agenda	63
19	We Don't Like to Be Proved Wrong	65
20	Open v Closed Questions	67
21	Agreeing and Disagreeing	69
22	Waiting	70
23	Understanding and Selling Questions	72
24	Take Notes	81
25	Secondary Questioning	82
26	Key Words and Clue Words	84
27	Budgets	86
28	Cialdini	88
29	The One-second Rule	89

30	Go for Small Orders	92
31	NLP (Neuro-Linguistic Programming)	94
32	Sell to the Woman – Close to the Man	96
33	Getting to 'Yes'	98
34	Three Yes Technique	99
35	Two Brochures	101
36	Correlations	102
37	Three Reasons	105
38	Forget the Concept of Loyalty	106
39	Deal with the Behaviour	108
40	Spare Tyre	115
41	Reciprocity	119
42	Competition	122
43	Windows of Opportunity	124
44	It Is Better Not to Do Something Than Do It Badly	126
45	Fake Your Attitude	127
46	Use Ballpark Figures	126
47	Implied v Explicit	130
48	Sell the Brand	133
49	Half Empty or Half Full	136
50	Commitment v Consistency	138
51	Use Letters of Intent	140
52	Do What You Say You Will Do	142
53	Give Bad News in Advance	143
54	Don't Upset Browsers	144
55	Never Say No	147
56	Control	149
57	Control, Influence and Concern	151
58	Comparison Theory	155
59	Quality v Price	158
60	Top-down Selling	161
61	Present Your Products in the Right Order	165
62	The Power of One	166
63	Testimonials	167
64	Avoid Pain	168
65	Sell 'Through People'	171

87 Practical Tips for Dynamic Selling

66	When to Sell Accessories	172
67	Don't Do What Others Do	173
68	Objections	174
69	The Third Most Powerful Word in Selling	180
70	Feel, Felt, Found	183
71	Get the Prospect to Sell the Product to You	185
72	Discounting	187
73	Fast, Good and Cheap	192
74	Break it to the Ridiculous	193
75	Cost v Price	194
76	Gestures	195
77	Decision Making	196
78	Four Differentiators	197
79	Trust the Customer	202
80	When to Close	205
81	Closing Techniques	206
82	Getting Your Next Appointment	209
83	Create an Objection	210
83a	Savers	213
84	Complaints	214
85	Dormant Accounts	218
86	Use Your results To Be the Best	219

Be the Best! **221**

Most salespeople know <u>what</u> they want to do

This guide shows <u>how</u> to do it

How to:

- stop prospects asking for a discount
- subtly control sales
- handle difficult objections
- make more money
- close customers who won't make a decision
- work to your strengths
- stop people from 'shopping around'
- protect business from competition
- avoid objections
- remain positive
- develop trust
- develop rapport
- get prospects to sell to you
- tell when people are disagreeing even if they seem to be agreeing
- get prospects to tell the truth
- convert prospects that are 'happy with their existing supplier'
- avoid price becoming an issue.

This book has also been designed as an excellent sales management tool. For example, if your sales team think think that people are price sensitive, get them to read the sections on price and differentiation. If they have a low order value, you may need to get them to study the section on discounting.

For Julie, Inga and Lindsay
You are always my inspiration

Introduction

I was sitting with Peter Wilson, the General Manager (Operations) of Reece Australia, at dinner one evening. We were discussing how to get salespeople to transfer learning from the training course to the workplace.

All of my clients want their salespeople to be good listeners and to ask the right questions. To be persistent at the right time. To be determined (like a dog with a bone) when there is a genuine opportunity. The trouble is, these characteristics can be found but they are rarely learned in a short training course. What Peter wanted is a way of getting ordinary salespeople to get more profitable sales.

'Practical Selling' was the answer but transferring it to the workplace required a tool. Peter had seen the improved sales and profit, but needed some way to 'keep it going'. He asked me to draw up a list of the ten most important practical tips for selling.

The idea for this book was born during that conversation. I couldn't decide which were the ten most important tips when I started to draw up a list. Peter looked at the first list and said, 'you know, if you keep going, you could have a best-seller from this list.'

What follows is a Sales Manager tool or a self-improvement tool. When you meet with a difficult challenge, the answer should be here.

As implied in the title of this book, I have concentrated on *practical* selling tips.

Winston Churchill said, 'nothing is ever achieved without a plan and no plan is ever achieved.' It is exactly the same with selling tips – no tip works and yet all tips work. Selling is not a perfect science and in fact, I believe, selling is an art rather than a science. This means you can do all the right things and get the wrong result and then you can do all the wrong things and get the right result.

Try all of the tips at some time and I am certain you will find they all work. Not every time, (if they did, you probably couldn't afford to buy the book – then again you probably couldn't afford not to buy the book!), but they work enough times to warrant learning and using them.

I have tried to put them in some sort of logical order. My logic was the sales sequence, e.g. the approach comes before establishing needs and so on. The best tips are not at the front with scraping the bottom of the barrel at the back! The reason is that delegates often say what was the best tip for them others will say is useless. Your 'best tip' could be anywhere.

I am a great believer in working to your own strengths and managing your weaknesses. I have included my Selling Styles Questionnaire so you can discover your strongest selling style and maximise your advantages. To get a free report on your selling style, follow the links from **http://www.practicalselling.co.uk/sellingstyles**

If only one of the techniques in this book works for you, then I am sure the book is of value. You will make more sales and more profit on each sale as a result. Try to focus on the tips that you can use. On sales training courses, I encourage delegates to focus on getting the one golden nugget rather than on tips they wouldn't use. It takes hard work to change a habit, even if you want to change the habit, and so I would recommend you focus on one tip at a time. Don't read this book! Just dip in and out, take one thing at a time, enjoy and prosper!

I believe every tip applies to every type of selling, I train salespeople from many disciplines from private bankers in Switzerland through to retail salespeople selling low cost items. It isn't always obvious how each tip applies but, with some imagination, it is possible to apply almost all tips to all selling.

One of the things you will notice is all the tips run into each other. For example, *Confirmation Bias* seems to operate in all tips, whether you are talking about 'Proving People Wrong' or 'Price v Quality'. This is entirely deliberate and really means most of the tips are practical applications of some basic principles. In my experience, the hardest thing to do is work out practical applications of techniques. The real value of this book is to allow you to implement all tips very quickly.

I do not advocate major behaviour or attitude change. I think these things are hard to achieve and take time. This is where most training fails. In essence, people don't change that much. Leopards don't change their spots. What I do advocate is that if you are a salesperson you use all the tools available to you. You wouldn't expect a surgeon to operate on you without knowing the techniques of surgery would you?

This book is packed with tools and techniques, many of which are very easy to implement, all of which I have used to increase my personal success, the success of my sales team and the sales of course delegates. Some of these increases have been dramatic.

In reading the book, you may get the impression I am sexist. I do believe women are to be envied. They are less violent, more family orientated and more intelligent (4% more) and they do better in schools! They are also better at reading body language and better managers in a crisis. Some of my best friends are women. I recommend reading Allan & Barbara Pease's book, *Why Men Don't Listen and Women Can't Read Maps!*. I do believe we are different and some of the tips reflect this.

Just a word on ethics. What I think is ethical, other people see as a bit dodgy and vice versa. I have included tips I have used and they have worked. I have also given tips I have seen others using and they work for them. I am making no moral judgements in terms of the tips. I have no doubt someone reading this book will feel some, most or even all of them, are unethical. I hope the use of them doesn't offend anyone. Because I cannot control your emotions (see tip no 57 – *Control, Influence, Concern*), please be assured that I am not worrying about it. You could send an email to **someonewhodoescare@blackhole.com**

Let me comment on research as well. I rarely believe any research unless it seems to make sense to me. Most research sets out to prove something and so is a little biased. I quote research and statistics throughout the book. I sometimes remember the source but not very often because the source is never that important to me. If you want to know the source of any piece of research, feel free to email me. Don't put 'Hi' in the subject line or my spam filter deletes it! My email address is at the back of the book.

I will try to find any research but my advice would be if you don't believe it, then you should make a decision whether you want to try it out. If you don't believe it and you don't want to try it, then the research is no use to you. Try to focus on some other aspect of the book that is of use to you.

It is often difficult to tell whether a writer is trying to be funny, is just stupid, or is insulting. As a general rule if you find anything amusing, I was trying to be funny! If you are offended, I was trying to be sensitive but failed! If you think I am stupid, I wasn't explaining that idea for your benefit, but for readers less astute than you!

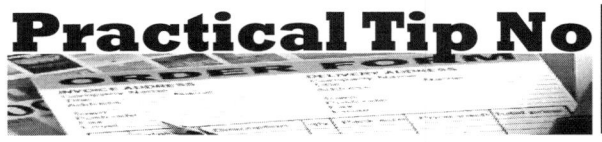

You Can't Fail

What I love about selling is you just can't fail. You go to see someone who isn't buying from you and you don't manage to sell to them. Have you failed? No – you have just found another way that doesn't work. There are probably thousands of ways not to sell. There are many ways *not to sell* to every customer and prospect. You just have to keep trying something different until you find the right way.

What amazes me about selling is that good salespeople seem to tinker with their selling all the time. The very fact that you are reading this book, or any sales book, is a good indication of your quality. Poor salespeople seem to consistently use the same tactics even when they know they don't work! 'Can I help you?' springs to mind.

In my first real job of hard selling I had left a profession to try selling which I didn't, at that time, recognise as a profession. I called on a prospect every six weeks for more than a year. He was one of the 17% that didn't buy (see tip no 40 – *Spare Tyre*).

After some time, he was getting fed up saying 'no' and he asked me why I kept calling. I was practising my skills – learning my trade. I figured if I was going to test new ways, I should test them on prospects, not on good customers. Every new thing I learned I took to him first. I figured if it would work on him, it would work on anyone.

Life is a series of lessons. If you don't learn the first time, the lesson keeps getting repeated until you do learn.

If it isn't working do something different.

15

Practical Tip No 2

Find Your Selling Style
(and use it!)

There are things people can do and do. There are things people can do but don't. There are things that people can't do but would. There are things that people can't do and wouldn't do.

So, I hope all that is clear then!

You have to focus on what *you can and would do*; not what you can't and won't do.

After many years of studying what makes a great Sales Professional, the inescapable conclusion is that there is no one effective style for selling. In fact four main styles can be identified, each of which can be equally effective. It was also noted that whilst most training was effectively geared towards 'fixing people's weaknesses', the most effective salespeople have an extreme style. It was also noted that some organisations and industries tend to gravitate towards one style.

There are two important dimensions that have a relative impact in a sale; these are the **product*** and the **relationship**.

I read lots of sales books. In almost all, the relationship between the salesperson and the customer is seen to be the 'magic key'. I have to disagree. I have had great relationships with some prospects that just couldn't or wouldn't buy from me for various reasons.

For some clients, the product is more important than the relationship and for some the relationship is more important than the product. When I go looking for a product, the last thing on my mind is finding a new best friend. I don't want a relationship and the salesperson that focuses on developing one with me is focused on their own needs rather than mine.

It is exactly the same for sales people. For some, the relationship is the most important – for others it is the product. The grid below identifies the selling styles and the notes illustrate the different ways in which these types successfully sell.

*Product

Many salespeople I have worked with tell me they don't sell 'products' they sell services or solutions etc. A dictionary definition of product is:

> **product** n. 1 thing or substance produced, esp. by manufacture. 2 result. 3 quantity obtained by multiplying. [Latin: related to produce]

When I talk about selling a product, this refers to the result of the sale for the buyer. What difference will your physical product, service or solution make to the client? How will their wealth be multiplied through using your solution?

17

If you understand your product to be the result obtained or the quantity obtained by multiplying, then you understand the need for benefits. Your selling perspective is directed and focused towards providing a benefit. The word 'product' applies whether you have a physical thing to sell or are selling a service.

To get a free report on your selling style log onto:
http://www.practicalselling.co.uk/
… and follow the directions.

How industries evolve

Industries can be identified as passing through four development phases:

- accuracy
- availability
- alteration
- advice.

Accuracy

Here is a new industry which is striving for accuracy. In other words, the main criterion for success is having a product that works and meets a required level of quality standard.

For example, the computer industry started with a few products, each striving to do what it promised it would do. Manufacturers needed to prevent hardware and software crashes and the selling focus was one of reliability. A strange marketing strategy, don't you think. Buy our product because when it breaks down you can press a button to connect to our help desk.

It is sad to say, but absolutely true, that some industries, or at least some companies, never come out of this phase!

Sales Professionals thrive in this environment.

Availability

As the market matures and so the products become a standard quality, then the industry may move towards a commodity market. Selling and marketing focus on influencing preferences. In this market, branding is one of the methods that manufacturers seek to differentiate between products that otherwise buyers may not see any differentiation in. For example tyre manufactures try to differentiate between brands when consumers see little differentiation.

The response of an organisation locked into this phase is either to create a differentiation or *pile 'em high and sell 'em cheap.*

Sales people without a strong style are best suited to this environment.

Alteration

One of the responses to avoid the Availability phase is to provide alterations. In this way, the manufacturers can customise the product to suit the buyers' needs thus providing a differentiation. For example, a manufacturer may have a basic product which you can customise by adding optional extras.

Relationship and Technical Experts are best suited to this environment

Advice

After alteration, there is a higher level to achieve which is Advice. Not only will the manufacturer or service provider alter their business modus operandi for the client but also they will investigate the client's way of working and suggest more productive uses for their products or services. In this way, the supplier becomes a business partner and attempts to maximise the business profit of the client rather than merely supply what is asked for.

Consultants are best suited to this environment

All markets start with **Accuracy** as the goal, although sometimes it is never achieved. As the market matures, there are two tracks to take, either the **Availability** track, or the **Alteration/Advice** track. The market may at any time revert to the Availability track and indeed, irrespective of the market decision, there may often be an availability track. No matter what the industry, there will always be someone who competes at the availability level. What they sell is no worse than anybody else. It may even pack in more features and benefits but it competes at the lower end of the price scale.

My tip is to determine your selling style and which phase your organisation competes in. Use the strengths of your style to increase your effectiveness.

Practical Tip No 3

Confirmation Bias

Understanding *confirmation bias* makes selling different and a lot easier.

First of all, let me explain confirmation bias then I will show how it affects your selling. When you understand confirmation bias you can then apply it to your advantage. You can also avoid the pitfalls of confirmation bias which causes a focus on the wrong aspects of selling.

Explanation

A psychologist (Watson) first coined the phrase confirmation bias in 1966 to describe a tendency of human behaviour.

> *'We seek to prove what we already believe to be true and ignore any evidence to the contrary.'*

What questions would you ask to find out if someone is an extrovert? Typically we would ask extrovert-loaded questions (do you enjoy going out, do you enjoy being with other people and so on) and ignore introvert-loaded questions (how much time do you spend on your own, how comfortable are you with your own company and so on). This is because we are seeking to prove something rather than disprove something.

Let me give you some practical examples of when confirmation bias applies.

If we believe a product is good quality, we look for evidence that we are correct and ignore any evidence to the contrary (magazine articles, friends recommendations).

If we believe something is inexpensive, we look for evidence that it is a low price and ignore any evidence that it isn't. Three shoppers

21

were asked which of three supermarkets they thought was the least expensive and then asked to shop in the three supermarkets. All shoppers bought goods which 'proved' their chosen supermarket was the least expensive.

If, as a salesperson, we believe a customer is a 'time-waster' or a 'tyre-kicker', then we look for evidence that we are right and ignore the evidence that few people come into our showroom with the sole intention of wasting the time of someone they have never met.

Another example of confirmation bias can been seen with mystery shopping – not a favourite of mine. Confirmation bias states that I search for evidence to prove me right. I have met many sales managers who conduct mystery shopping studies and they are equally convinced they are right to do mystery shop reports.

I was at a dinner party one evening and a fellow guest asked me what I did for a living. When I told her, she asked if I could tell her what a mystery shopper is? She had been shopping that day and the salesperson accused her of being one – even though she didn't even understand the term!

So, what is 'mystery shopping'? Some organisations pay 'actors' to act as prospects! They then provide a report on the performances of the salespeople.

Let me give the 'evidence' that I have collected to support my case that mystery shopping is overused and overrated.

1. If you introduce mystery shopping into your organisation you will find the very best salespeople often having the worst mystery shopping reports. This happens because:
    a) we have little idea what the very best salespeople do that makes them so good (see tip no 2 – *Find your Selling Style*)
    b) good salespeople seem to work out that the 'prospect' is not a serious buyer and tend to filter them out as not being a genuine prospect. This happens even when the mystery shopper 'buys'. Some companies get the mystery shopper to actually make a purchase if they are treated correctly. The purchase is reimbursed.
    c) Even if they purchase something, I believe, because of what

psychologists term 'non-verbal leakage' (sounds awful doesn't it!), their body language leaks the message that they are not serious buyers.

2. Shopping is not a one way thing. Salespeople don't do the same to everyone – they react to situations. The mystery shopping report tells of one interaction on one day between two people. If a second mystery shopper came moments after, they would undoubtedly get treated differently.

3. Why are you paying someone to do the job of the sales manager? If the sales manager doesn't know how 90% of prospects are being treated, you have committed the cardinal sin of sales management. You have allowed the sales manager to get too far away from the salespeople. You have probably given the sales manager an office to help him!

4. Mystery shopping seems to be used as a way of catching people doing things wrongly. I know this is not inevitable but common sense is not common practice. I have yet to see the organisation using mystery shopping in a positive way. My evidence for this is talking to the salespeople about mystery shopping – most hate it!

5. When salespeople start accusing genuine customers of being mystery shoppers, you have focused people on entirely the wrong aspect. They are more focused on not making mistakes than taking risks and getting sales.

My advice if you do use mystery-shoppers would be:

1. Divert the amount spent into training the right behaviour rather than checking up on your salespeople.
2. Never let a salesperson see a mystery shop report. If you must – use it as a management tool for telling you where you need to go with training.
3. The acting ability is critical – get them to mystery shop you first!

4   Do your own job properly before working on the salespeople. Try finding out how hard it is for your customers (internal and external) to deal with you first. Train the salespeople to deal with prospects correctly. Monitor the salespeople by observation, not just for one mystery shopper, but everybody they deal with.
5   Judge salespeople by their results not by your perception of how they are doing the job.
6   Use information which is readily available to determine how shoppers are treated. Closing ratios against the number of people receiving a pitch. Compare region against region and area against area. Read customer complaints (and complimentary letters).

I recently came across the most extreme example of confirmation bias ever. The company I was working with is probably one of the best companies I work with. They are tremendously successful. In four years, they went from second largest to the biggest supplier in their industry. That involved increasing their sales by over 300% in a four-year period.

They are very well organised and have profitability figures most companies would envy. How could confirmation bias affect them?

Well they decided to diversify from trade sales to sell through showrooms direct to the public. The only trouble was they found that initially people just wanted to come in to the showroom to 'have a look'. In short, their salespeople convinced them the public were 'time-wasters'.

Their response was to prevent people coming in to the showroom unless they had an appointment. Unbelievable as it may seem, they were convinced these people didn't want to buy and they proved it to themselves. Luckily, you don't grow like they have without being intelligent!! They spotted a signal (falling sales) and started to encourage anyone to come into the showroom.

Confirmation bias makes selling relatively straightforward. In essence if you find out what people already believe and then confirm it, they will believe you because of confirmation bias.

Let me take confirmation bias on to a more important topic. How important do you think price is in the decision to buy? On courses, the responses I get are generally in the 30% – 90% range. I have had people say it is 100%.

Confirmation bias suggests that if you believe price to be very important in the buying decision, you will seek evidence to prove you are right and ignore any evidence to the contrary.

Manchester Business School conducted a study which showed that price was just 8% of the decision to buy. Of course, because of confirmation bias, you may be thinking, 'perhaps, but not in my industry, my products, our market place, current economic conditions etc'. What you are doing is seeking evidence which proves you are right and ignoring the evidence that you are wrong. The evidence that price cannot be important is staring you in the face.

Would you like some evidence?

Evidence No. 1:

Suppose we wrote to your customers who buy from you at the moment and asked them: *'How many of you are too stupid to find someone with lower prices than us?'* or *'Do you think you could find cheaper products than ours?'*

What percentage of customers would say they think that your company is the cheapest in the market place? Most customers know you are not the cheapest. Most have a perception that the internet will be cheaper even though it often isn't. Yet we ignore this evidence (and I am about to give you lots of evidence).

Evidence No. 2:

If price were important, would it be possible to sell a product that you can get for free? In most countries I work in, you can walk up to any tap and get drinking water for free – yet bottled water is sold in all countries I work in. If you ask people why they buy bottled water, this is what they will say.

Number one reason is because of *taste*. If I do a taste test, I can predict that most people will choose tap water. All I have to do is use chilled tap water and slightly warm bottled water. Water is actually tasteless, although there is some taste to the minerals etc. People decide 'best taste' of water on the basis of temperature.

Number two reason people give is for *health reasons.* Some bottled water is actually less healthy than normal tap water. The water authorities add things like fluoride for health reasons and bottled water has much of the mineral content filtered out.

In March 1999, in a study of 103 brands of bottled water, the Natural Resources Defence Council found that bottled water was no more safe than tap water. A third of the brands contained arsenic and E Coli and a quarter were merely bottled tap water.

Drinkers of Perrier may remember a scandal that Perrier (allegedly – details of my solicitor on request!) contained anti-freeze (ethylene glycol)! Maybe that is so that the temperature of the water can be lower and therefore will taste better. I am sure they don't now because the very, very nice people at Perrier have made sure it is anti-freeze free. I am sure they now have one of the best, healthiest water on sale!

Have you ever wondered why one of the best selling bottled water on the market place is called Evian and that backwards spells 'naive' Is this just a coincidence?

I have also seen bottled water which says 'this water has been filtered through the Grampian Mountains of Scotland for millions of years – use by Sept 30th!!

Coca-Cola launched a bottled water called Dansani. They used Thames water. Do you remember the 'Only Fools & Horses' episode where they sold 'Peckham Spring Water'? Similar thing. Thames water costs about 0.3 pence per litre. Dansani was 95p per half litre. Coca-Cola withdrew Dansani because it contained higher than permitted levels of bromate! So what if bromate is carcinogenic? Profits have to be made haven't they?

Evidence No. 3:
If price were important, wouldn't the biggest companies be the cheapest? Most often the biggest companies are also the most expensive.

Evidence No. 4
If price were important, all salespeople would get the same results or at least the sales people with the lowest margins would have the highest volumes and vice versa. This doesn't happen. Good salespeople have high volumes and high margins. It isn't the price that is driving their results – it is what they are doing.

Evidence No. 5
If price were important, you would only have one supplier of everything because we would go to the cheapest.

Evidence No. 6
These days, even something so mundane as the name on the label seems to be more important than the price. This is why brand names are so important. Or maybe someone can explain to me why (according to Naomi Klein in 'No Logo') Nike can charge £20 for a hat that costs them pennies to make.

So, why do people think price is more important than it is? Part of the reason is *confirmation bias*. We believe price is important when we buy and therefore it must be important.

I will explain why I think this happens. If you look at tips nos. 6 and 7, you will find we ask 'why' at the wrong time, and place enormous importance on the answers. Most sales managers I know are desperate to find out why people are *not buying* from them. In fact, if you go to your sales manager and say you have made the follow-up calls for today, you have spoken to three prospects and they have all decided not to buy from you, my bet is he will ask you why they didn't buy from you.

I believe human beings are very clever. Because the word 'why' is an aggressive word, I played a game with my children that I called the five why smack. The rules of this game were quite easy, if they asked me five 'whys' consecutively, I would smack them. The fourth answer was because I told you so! My children used to say 'Why?', 'Why?', 'Why?', 'Why?'... ... 'How come?' We are very clever and learn quickly, so if my boss is going to ask me why people don't buy from me, I learn to ask customers first.

87 Practical Tips for Dynamic Selling

When I ask what percentage of the decision to buy is based on price, what most people immediately think of is what percentage of people DON'T buy because of price.

If you ask someone why they don't buy from you, more than 80% of people give the same reason – 'Price'. Yet we know price is not a big factor in the decision to buy. People often use it as a decision not to buy. If you follow up people that say they didn't buy because of price, you will find that many actually bought something that is more expensive. What is happening here is that prospects give a reason for not buying that is not in your control. Very few people will criticise you personally.

I would recommend not asking people why they didn't buy from you. Many salespeople I train feel uncomfortable with this because they feel if they can find out why people are not buying they have some tools for the future. I agree with this to an extent and if asking people why they don't buy were an effective method of getting accurate information, I would support it. The difficulty is that I am certain that, for the most part, people answering this question give logical, non-personal reasons rather than the emotional, personal reasons that I believe are the real reasons.

If you want to find out why people don't buy from you, perhaps you could try asking them why they *did* buy from someone else. What did your competitor do for them that they liked? I am still not certain you will get accurate reasons here. Many people will give reasons associated with the product and service, many will say just because they were cheaper. Rather than saying, 'They were cheaper,' most customers say, 'They gave me a great deal.' When you investigate this, it wasn't cheaper, but they felt they had received a discount which made it better value. A friend told me recently that he lost a contract to instal double glazing. Everest gave the customer a 'great deal' (the customer's words). Everest got £9,000 rather than his quote of £2,700, yet the customer's perception was that Everest had given them a better deal. The greed of a discount is often more important than the price (see *Price v Quality*).

Some will give reasons related to the personal treatment by the salesperson but because there is an implied criticism of you in here,

87 Practical Tips for Dynamic Selling

many people will avoid this. Hence my recommendation that if people choose not to buy from you, thank them for considering you and giving you the chance, and then try to ignore anything they say.

The side benefit to this is you get less negative feedback and I have always found that less negative feedback improves my performance.

Although we seem to always ask people why they don't buy from us, the opposite is also the case. We rarely ask people why they do buy from us. I have always found this strange. Why do we place more emphasis on feedback which is negative than feedback which is positive? (See tip no 64 – *Avoid Pain*) The reason for buying from a supplier is often linked to the service provided by the supplier. Who is in a better position to judge how much the additional service you provide is worth? The person that is buying from you and has experienced your service or the person that has never bought from you and therefore hasn't experienced your service.

Always ask existing customers and new customers why they decided to buy from you. Guess what people say. If you ask someone why they bought from you, more than 50% will mention you personally. They will give you positive feedback about what you personally do. They will also show you where you should focus your selling style. For example, people will say because of your knowledge, or because of the length of time you spent with them and so on.

Now, I ask you, what is more important for you to know? Why people don't buy from you or where you are stronger than your competitors and where they are deficient?

You will find that people will mention price as well, around 8% will say because you were the cheapest (hence the Manchester Business School study). Many more people will say 'you weren't the cheapest but ...'

A word of caution here. 'Why?' is a very aggressive word and you should never start a sentence with it. If a customer says, 'okay, I will take six of them,' and you say, 'Why?' they may well respond 'okay, I will only take three of them.' 'Why?' 'okay, I won't bother taking any!'

I recommend saying something like 'Thank you very much for your business. I want to make certain everything goes in accordance with your expectations, would you mind if I asked why you chose to buy from us?

Cold Calling Techniques that Really Work!

Preparation List

1. Establish your unique selling points in your mind.
2. Write down 10 opening questions referring to the above list.
3. Dare to be different.
4. Be creative.
5. Prepare three questions that you would expect to elicit three yes answers.
6. Don't plan to do business. Plan only to find out what the client needs.
7. Tune out the world.
8. Be a shareholder – really try to improve the client's business.
9. You get more appointments at unusual times, and quarter to the hour is better than quarter past.

Check List

1. Did the opening break the client's preoccupation with what he was doing?
2. Did the opening make the client want to listen?
3. Did the opening excite the client?
4. Did the opening put the client at ease?
5. Did the opening make him feel important?

6. Did the opening set the scene?
7. Was the opening pre-planned?
8. Have you written it down?
9. Have you practised it?
10. Did you obtain the client's name before launching in to your spiel?
11. Did you use it often?
12. If you were asking for an appointment, did you have a firm reason why you were asking?
13. Did you use the word 'because' when you were asking for an appointment?
14. Did your opening statement include a benefit for the client?
15. Did you smile while you were delivering the opening?
16. Did you sound enthusiastic?
17. Did you obtain three 'yes' answers at the beginning?

Word Power

Words are critical. Albert Mehrabian said that we communicate 55% through non-verbal means (body language), 38% through our tone and only 7% through the words that we speak.

I think this misses the most vital part of communication. The most important thing is the perception of the receiver. Have you ever been taken the wrong way?

I do an exercise on courses where I walk up to someone and say:

'Congratulations, I hear you have just been promoted. I don't have time at the moment but could I give you a call later and we will go out for a beer to celebrate.'

I then ask the group about what they think of me. Normally some people see me as being very sincere, very friendly and they are sure I will go out for a beer to celebrate. Others see me as being very patronising, in too much of a hurry to get away and very unlikely to go for a beer.

All the delegates heard the same words, they heard them in exactly the same order and the same tone. They also saw the same body language. All three aspects of Mehrabian's communication were the same for everybody and yet two entirely opposing views come out. This can only be because a more important aspect of communication is how one consciously or subconsciously chooses to *perceive* the communication.

Another more important aspect of communication is prior knowledge, for example, in the above scenario, if you knew I was a friend. I may even have recommended the person for the promotion. It would be difficult to conclude from my conversation that I was anything but sincere *and* in a hurry.

If you knew that I was a rival for the promotion and I thought that

87 Practical Tips for Dynamic Selling

I was sure to get the promotion and bitterly disappointed I didn't get it, in this case, it is more likely that you would conclude that I was insincere.

Sadly, other people's choices on perception and prior knowledge cannot be controlled (see tip no 57 – *Control, Influence, Concern*) and so it is pointless worrying about it. What you can do when you have been misunderstood, is consider it from the position of prior knowledge and perception.

I also think that the words used are far more important than Mehrabian perceived. If you ask the defence secretary what impact it would have if we changed the name of his ministry to 'The Killing Department' or 'The Attack Department' I would think the public's entire perception would change!

Marketing has shown just how important words are – entire product ranges have failed because of single words. Ask Opel cars about the success of the Opel Nova in Spain (*No va* means 'doesn't work' in Spanish!) How about the Ford Pinto in Brazil. *Pinto* in Portuguese means a small willie!

Tip no 4 is to choose your words very carefully. Because 'greed' and 'fear' are big motivators (see tip no 64) the word 'FREE' is still the most powerful in marketing. All proposals and pitches should appeal to the client's fear and greed.

So let us look at some critical words in selling.

Practical Tip No 6

Know When to *Avoid* the Most Dangerous Word in Selling

The most *powerful* word in selling is the word 'Why'. The most *dangerous* word in selling is, coincidentally, the word 'Why'. When you ask someone 'Why?' it is seen as a challenge and causes people to justify their remark. It is also a very aggressive question.

When to avoid

This means you should never use the word 'Why' when anything negative is said. You may recognise you are almost pre-programmed to do just that.

For example, when the prospect says; *'I don't like your widgets/ service or whatever'*, most people would ask 'why?' (or how come?) immediately. If you do, it is almost impossible to sell your widgets to this prospect. What you have done is challenged them and caused them to justify that remark. It therefore follows that they will give you all the reasons why they don't like your widgets. They rarely say anything positive about your widgets.

- In order now to sell to them you have to convince them they are wrong (see tip no 19 – *We don't like to be proved wrong*).

- If anything negative is said, you should focus on what the prospect *does* want, not what they *don't* want.

- In response to the statement *'I don't buy that widget from you'*, you could ask *'What must the perfect widget have for your needs?'* or *'What would the perfect supplier of widgets have to do for you?'*

Examples of negative things said:

'I don't buy ... from you.'
'I don't like your ...'
'I prefer to buy those from your competitor.'
'I decided to buy from someone else.'
'I am not going ahead.'
'You are too expensive.'
'I don't like the colour.'
'I don't like that feature.'

In all of these cases, you must avoid asking 'why?' Focus on what the perfect product or solution would have.

Practical Tip No 7

Know When to *Use* the Most Powerful Word in Selling

When you should ask 'why?'

A word of caution before we begin. The word 'why' is aggressive and therefore you should never use it at the beginning of a sentence. Disguise it in the middle of a sentence.

You should always ask why, *when anything positive is said.* You may also notice we seem to be pre-programmed not to ask why in these situations.

For example, someone says, *'I would prefer to deal with you'.* Asking them 'why?' causes them to justify the remark. Because you want to disguise the word in the sentence you may ask, *'That is really interesting – would you mind if I asked you why that is?'* They will now tell you many reasons why they prefer to deal with you. This has the impact of making it harder for them to negotiate on price (see tip no 73 – *Fast, Good and Cheap*). It also means if your competitor contacts them, they will be resistant to changing since that would involve proving them to be wrong (see tip no 19 – *We don't like to be proved wrong*).

Asking the question 'why?' at the *right* times will help prevent buyers' remorse (when purchasers start wondering if they have made the right decision). It increases loyalty and avoids price negotiations.

Examples of positive things said

'I only buy xyz from you.'
'I prefer your xyz.'

'I prefer to buy those from you.'
'That sounds good.'

Any buying signal

A word of caution

'I need to think about it' has to be treated carefully with regard to asking 'why?'. As a salesperson, you would like them to think about it. In this circumstances, asking 'why?' may produce good results. The difficulty is this statement is sometimes used as a smokescreen for a hidden objection. Asking 'why?' in these circumstances would be counter productive.

See tip no 11 for strategies for dealing with 'I need to think about it'.

Practical Tip No 8

Use the Second Most Powerful Word in Selling

The word 'because' is the second most powerful word in selling. Learn to use it and your sales will grow. There are two different times you should use the word 'because'.

When you are asking someone to do something

In his book *'Influence – The Science and Practice'*, Robert Cialdini showed an experiment in which the success of getting agreement was increased by 34% simply because the word 'because' was used in the sentence.

This is because people like to have a reason for doing things.

Any time you ask someone to do something, always use the word 'because' in the sentence because they are more likely to do it.

Examples:

'Can we arrange a meeting for next week, because I would like to find out about your needs?'
'Can you sign here because I can check the stock is available?'
'You need to pay a deposit of 20% because we have to hold the stock for you'

When giving your opinion

Anytime you are giving your opinion, you should use the word 'because' in the sentence because then you are giving your professional expertise rather than your opinion.

'I think this one is better for you because...........'
'I don't think we could do that because..............'
'I think this is a better quality product because...........'

Any time you use the word 'think' in a sentence, you should also use the word 'because'.

Practical Tip No 9

Problem v Concern

Problem

A dictionary definition of problem is:

problem n. doubtful or difficult matter requiring a solution.

Often customers will not perceive they have a problem because they already have a solution. When the oil industry was maturing in Scotland, if something went wrong they would often fly an engineer out to the oil rigs. Did they have a problem? No! They already had a solution.

If you were selling them a fax machine (which at that time was just hitting the market place and cost several thousands of pounds) asking about problems may not uncover the need. By faxing a diagram of the problem, an engineer could often diagnose and draw a solution. This could be faxed back and fixed by people on board the rig. Fax machines saved many thousands of pounds.

I first became aware of using *problem or concern* when I was a corporate insurance broker. I was looking for prospects that had a minimum spend of £1 million in corporate (non-life) insurance. I devised an approach to companies which was very successful (it isn't easy to phone the biggest companies in the market and arrange an appointment with the MD!).

One prospect I contacted me invited me to speak to them and I duly met the MD. I asked what 'problems' they were having with their existing insurance broker and they told me they didn't have any problems. They wanted to know about the fabulous new scheme I had devised. The conversation moved to other aspects and we met several times. They came to our offices and met the corporate broking staff who would look after them. They also met with our management.

87 Practical Tips for Dynamic Selling

My manager asked if they had any *concerns* about their existing brokers. They told him of an outstanding claim they had. They were a company of Marine Engineers and had a contract to do some welding on a ship that was in dry dock.

Unfortunately, one of those everyday mishaps that befall you from time to time happened – they set fire to the ship, causing £1.5 million pounds of damage to it. Still that wasn't a problem, they had liability insurance didn't they? Well actually no they didn't!

They should have had liability insurance, but it was a very hard market for liability insurance and their insurers had written to their brokers refusing to renew their policy! The brokers had been trying to arrange alternative cover and had been unable to. They were left uninsured (and uninformed!) for one weekend. A guy called Murphy predicted (correctly as it happens) that on that very weekend, they would set light to a ship! I am sure you get the idea!

The point was, *they weren't prepared to disclose problems until they had developed sufficient trust level.*

I am not certain whether using the word concern earlier would have helped in that extreme situation. Since then, I developed my own use of 'concern' and I am certain (although it is impossible to measure) it has helped many, many times over.

I have found if you ask prospects about their *problems*, you restrict it to things that they cannot find a solution for. Asking what *concerns* them produces much better results.

I guess this is probably influenced by the implications (see tip no 47 – *Implied v Explicit*) that if they have a problem they are incompetent. If they have concerns it implies they are diligent.

41

Practical Tip No 10

Coach v Help

People don't like asking for help.

To ask for help means I am helpless and (particularly men) don't like to admit they are helpless.

I was running a course recently when a delegate turned up 15 minutes late. He apologised and then told me he was actually in the same street as the hotel one hour before the course started. I asked him what happened and he said he must have missed the hotel. He had driven around looking for the hotel for one hour rather than ask someone for help!

This is one reason why the approaches *'Can I help you?'* or even *'How can I help you?'* are not brilliant. Another reason is because these invoke Reciprocity (see tip no 41). If you help them, they feel under an obligation to buy.

Any sentence you use in an approach in retail selling that includes the word 'help' is provoking a response that will include the word 'looking'.

When running a course one day, a delegate said they approached every customer and prospect and asked, *'Can I help you?'* It never caused him a problem. I asked what he did and he told me he was responsible for incoming telesales. That was the reason! When you answer the phone with, *'Can I help you?'* not many people will respond, *'No thanks, I am just looking'*!

Because sales trainers and consultants focus on the concept of not asking, 'Can I help you?', I have noticed that, 'How can I help you?' is being used by everyone, e.g. hotel receptionists, telephone answering agencies and so on. I personally believe it doesn't make a blind bit of difference in these situations! I am not saying here that you should stop it. If it works for you then keep doing it.

So, one aspect of using the word 'help' is to avoid asking others if

87 Practical Tips for Dynamic Selling

you can 'help' them. There are better approaches – see tip no 16 – *Approach in the Right Way*.

Another aspect is when you are asking others to help you. If you ask them to help you, it is simply saying that you are helpless. It is much better if you ask someone to coach you rather than to help you. Use phrases such as:

- 'Would you mind coaching me through your authorisation procedures for purchasing?
- 'Would you mind coaching me through your organisation chart?

You will be surprised how many clients will help you to sell to them if you ask, 'Would you coach me through how you would go about increasing our business with your company?'

In all these circumstances, 'coach' implies you have some skills which need direction. 'Help' means you can't do it without them. Because of this, I think you get much better responses to the 'coach'-type question.

If you ask a telephonist to help you, then you must use commitment (see tip no 50). Most people say, 'Can you help me?' and then go on without waiting for a response. Leave a gap so the person commits to helping (coaching) you before proceeding.

In section 12, we consider user buyers, economic buyers and technical buyers. It is especially important to ask user buyers if they can coach you through selling to the economic and technical buyers.

Practical Tip No 11

Think

I found a strong correlation between salespeople who rarely ask what the customers are thinking, and getting the statement or objection, *'I need to think about it.'*

If you continually ask people what they are thinking, they find it very difficult to object using *'I need to think about it'*. If they have been doing all their thinking out loud, it doesn't make sense to claim that they need to think about it.

You should vary the way you ask about thinking.

'How do you feel about that?'
'How would that suit?'
'How do you think that would meet your needs?'
'Do you think that is what you are looking for?'

'Think' and 'feel' are perfect words to use in trial closes. *'How do you think that would work for you?' 'Do you feel this would suit you?'*

Let's look at the statement: 'I need to think about it'.

When I hear it, I know I haven't used the word 'think' often enough with this customer. However, the horse has bolted and trying to close the door is a waste of time.

Asking 'why?' or 'what do they need to think about?' can be counter-productive.

It is a statement – not an objection. It is not a good strategy to interrupt their thinking with your talking. The one-second rule (tip no 29) is your first port of call.

If that doesn't produce meaningful results, then use an empathy statement (tip no 68 – *Objections*) and reciprocity (tip no 41)

Practical Tip No 12

Sell What is Personally Important

Having said that price is not important, let's look at three different types of buyer as identified by Miller Heiman in the excellent book – *Strategic Selling*. In small businesses, these types of buyers may be combined so that they are in just one or two people. In very large businesses, there may be many people that make up the buyers. For example you may have a whole department that are technical buyers.

The Economic Buyers

The economic buyer's role is to screen out – they sign the cheques, and they can say they will *not* buy something. They can choose which supplier they will buy from, but they cannot say they will buy something. A definitive quality of pure economic buyers is that they do not choose the product, someone else specifies what they need. For example, this may be a purchasing department. They can tell you that there is no budget to buy what you want, but they don't go to technical departments and say we are going to buy this for you. The technical department or the user must place the request first.

The Technical Buyers

The technical buyer specifies what the product must have and what it must not have. They set the criteria of the product to be purchased. An example of this would be a research department, a quality control department, architects and so on.

The User Buyers

The user buyer actually uses or installs the product.

In selling, there are five things that are important to these buyers, (the relationship may have some importance to many buyers, but I want to leave that aside for a moment and look at the other four factors.

45

In a sale you have:

- a relationship (which we will ignore for the purposes of this exercise)
- the price
- the features of the product
- the benefits of the product
- the convenience of buying the product.

The price
The price is self-explanatory.

The features
I consider *features* to be facts that no one would disagree with. It is a feature of a car that it has four wheels, or ABS braking system, or airbags. No one would disagree with a feature; it either has them or hasn't got them.

The benefits
The *benefits* of a product is what you think the feature will do for you. As a result, people can (and do) argue with them. For example, the benefit of ABS Braking System may be that it makes the car safer for the driver. People argue with this and some studies have shown that ABS has caused an increase in accidents and injuries. For this reason some modern cars are made with active ABS (it can be switched off).

It is a benefit of airbags that they protect you from injury. Again people argue with this as airbags sometimes cause injury (particularly broken jaws). Again, some modern cars are being designed with active airbags (which only half inflate at low speeds and for heavier drivers, or when sitting close to the steering wheel).

The convenience
The *convenience* of a product I am talking about here is how easy it is to purchase. The quality of your brochures, the information in your catalogues, is your ordering system easy to use and do your prospects understand how to use it.

87 Practical Tips for Dynamic Selling

Some products have convenience aspects that are actually benefits. For example, you can buy 'snap on' (the feature) plumbing fittings which are quicker to fit (the benefit). Some plumbers would argue about the benefits saying you get more comebacks and they don't save time. The aspect of convenience I am considering in this exercise is only meant to be the convenience of buying.

A practical exercise

What I would like you to do is rank the four factors according to importance for each of the three different types of buyer. For example, you may think for the Economic buyer, convenience is most important, features next, then benefits and finally price (but you would be wrong!!)

Rank - [P]rice, [F]eatures, [B]enefits and [C]onvenience	Most important	Second most important	Third most important	Least important
The Economic Buyer				
The Technical Buyer				
The User Buyer				

Try this exercise before turning over to see my answers

47

The Economic Buyer

| The Economic Buyer | C | P | B | F |

    Most Important is   CONVENIENCE
    Second most important   PRICE
    Third most Important is   BENEFITS
    Least important   FEATURES

Convenience is the most important thing when selling to an Economic buyer. There are many examples of this. Economic buyers never go out and research the market for the best product or the lowest price; we have to go to them. A builder involved in a project will employ a plumber. The builder is effectively the Economic buyer. They know that if they purchase the products they could save money. They know that the project plumber adds a margin to the materials purchase but it is much more convenient for them to pass on the responsibility to the plumber.

In banking, the Economic buyer would often be the client. They know they could research the market without employing a financial advisor but it is more convenient to get someone else to do it. Convenience has an impact on the Price v Cost. By making it easier they are also reducing their actual and emotional cost, i.e. it takes out stress, etc.

When I was taught to sell, the Economic buyer seemed to be the most important and you had to find out who was the economic buyer. Consequently, I found sales training to be more geared towards negotiation which is where you will head if you sell only to Economic buyers.

Having said that relationship is important to some buyers, I worked for an organisation whose prices were way above any competitor. Our most competitive product in terms of price was at least five times more expensive than any competitor. Some Economic buyers used to dislike me. It didn't matter that I tried to do to develop a relationship. They still had to buy if I did my job correctly with the Technical Buyer and the User Buyer!!

87 Practical Tips for Dynamic Selling

In today's environment of empowerment, you should recognise that the *user buyer* is the most important to your sale. It doesn't matter if the Economic buyer wants to buy from you, and the Technical buyer has specified your product. If the User buyer refuses to use the product, then you can never get a repeat order.

You must find out who the user buyers are, get access to them and sell to them. Most companies have small 'give-aways' – pens and such like. Most salespeople use them with the Economic buyers but I say they should be given to the User buyers.

In order to sell to an Economic buyer, you must use the User buyers. Fortunately, there is something to help you.

You have invested a lot of time with the users to make sure yours is the right product. The user(s) make their request to the purchasing department and they call you in for a discussion. You are now in an entirely different ball game.

The Economic buyer now is only interested in price. They are talking about *'sharpening pencils'*, *'going to the market place'*, *'tendering process'*, *'due diligence'* etc. You need the inside help of the user buyers to complete the sale with the maximum advantage to you.

In this scenario, you can exploit the situation that in most organisations there is conflict between the Users and the Economic buyers. Most salespeople I know don't like the Economic buyers in this situation. Usually the Users dislike the Economic buyers even more than you do!

Economic buyers are known by users as people that buy the cheapest rather than giving them the brand they really need.

The Economic buyers have the rough task of keeping the stock levels such that the Users always have stocks. With the best will in the world, they have an impossible job. Who does the user blame for not ordering in time – themselves or perhaps they blame the system? No, they have a tendency to blame the poor Economic buyer.

My tip is to go back to the User buyers and tell them of your difficulty with the Economic buyers. Ask them to coach (see tip no 10) you through selling to them.

When asking for leads or referrals, here is a question that works well. *'You have a lot of knowledge of this company/industry. If you*

87 Practical Tips for Dynamic Selling

were in my position, how would you go about selling more products?'

This is especially effective when used with reciprocity (see tip no 41). You will be surprised how many people coach you into selling to them.

I have said that the Features are the least important to the Economic buyer – let me explain why.

First, we don't like paying for something we don't need or want. I bought a mobile telephone and the salesman proudly told me it had a camera on the back. I didn't want the camera. His response? 'You don't have to use it!' That missed the point, I don't want to pay for something I don't want.

Second, the Economic buyer hears all the features and thinks this is more expensive than necessary.

Third, more features mean more to go wrong. There are more complex training requirements and so on. In our company, our economic buyer was set against buying our preferred telephone system because it was too complex. Of course, because we were the Users, we got the complex one. It was so complex, nobody could even transfer a call from one extension to another! One colleague set the telephone alarm but couldn't work out how to stop it from working every day at the same time!

Fourth, suppose there is a choice between three products that all cost £1,000. Product 1 has 10 features, product 2 has 5 features and product 3 has 3 features.

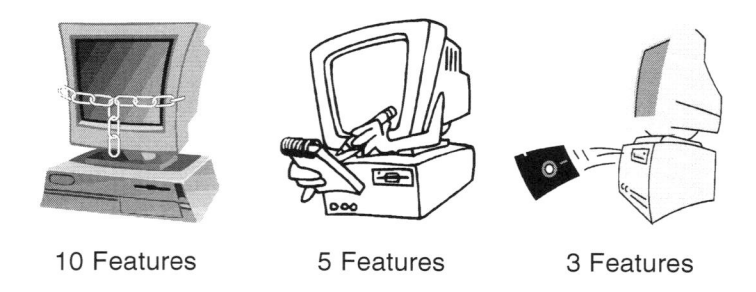

10 Features   5 Features   3 Features

The Economic buyer will conclude product 3 is the best quality. In product 1 each feature appears to be worth £100, in product 2 £200,

87 Practical Tips for Dynamic Selling

in product 3 £333. Hence product 3 is the best quality.

What is strange about this is that when you listen to the arguments of a salesperson with an Economic buyer, they tend to be feature based. 'Yes, ours is more expensive but it has ... (all features).' You should never try to argue with an Economic buyer using features. Use tips nos. 73 & 75 (*Fast, Good and Cheap* and *Cost v Price*). Better still, get User & Technical buyers to support you and get them to sell to the Economic buyer.

When you approach the Users and Technical buyers, ask them which product they prefer (assuming it is your product!) and then ask them, 'Why do you prefer it?' (see tip no 7 – *When to Use the most powerful word in selling*). Asking them 'Why?' commits them to a position and they will defend their decision, finding it much harder to back down.

The Technical Buyer

The Technical Buyer	C	F	B	P

Most Important is   CONVENIENCE
Second most important   FEATURES
Third most Important is   BENEFITS
Least important   PRICE

Most groups I work with chose Features first for the Technical buyer. Let me explain why Convenience is actually more important. Imagine an architect who specifies bathroom products. How much chance do you have of getting your product specified if they don't use your catalogue? The answer is slightly less chance than a cat in a hot place!

Take engineers who are specifying electronic components. They normally only specify from catalogues they are familiar with. That is also the reason former practice was to specify only one product in the first place! If they specified two, they had to test two. Commercial pressures caused this practice to change, so now acceptable alternative products are also usually specified.

For this reason, I say when you are trying to get your product

51

87 Practical Tips for Dynamic Selling

specified by a Technical buyer, your objective is to become the 'Catalogue of Choice'.

To do this:

1. Never take a catalogue with you into an appointment with them! Your first job is to find out:
   a) Do they know where your catalogue is? If they don't, you can't be specified!
   b) How often do they use it? Is it in pristine condition or well thumbed?
   c) How familiar are they with it? Can they find things easily? Ask them to find some technical information on some pretext (you don't want to appear to be 'testing' them).

2. Do a catalogue presentation to anyone that is not 100% okay on the above.
   a) Show them how your catalogue is organised, sell the benefits of the catalogue. Show them how comprehensive the catalogue is. Take something they would search for frequently and show them how to quickly find the information in your catalogue. (I always think I should use a split infinitive here! I mean the specifier should find it quickly not that you should show them quickly!)
   b) Focus on the products you would like them to specify. Go for your strongest products and your best chance products.
   c) Focus on their problem products. What do they find it hard to specify? Remember if convenience is a big driver if you make it easier, they will specify.

3. Do a catalogue presentation to everyone even if they are 100% okay on the above. This time, you need to focus on products they don't buy from you. Customers tend to put you in boxes (see tip no 43 – *Windows of Opportunity*). Always be looking to extend the range of your products they use. Focus on the ease of using the catalogue for these products as well as showing how much better your products are.

For Technical buyers, salespeople tend to focus on the features of the products and how much better they are than competitors. That is largely irrelevant if they find it too hard to specify them.

The User Buyer

The User Buyer	C	B	F	P

    Most Important is   CONVENIENCE
    Second most important   BENEFITS
    Third most Important is   FEATURES
    Least important   PRICE

I can often demonstrate on courses how convenience is the most important for a user buyer. How many delegates would attend a sales training course if it was voluntary. I am sure *you* would; you are taking the time to read this book! You want to improve your skills and are prepared to pay the price for doing so. Most delegates only attend because their boss forces them to. If the invite said please attend if you have nothing better to do, how many would attend?

    The major thing to note is that you should never discuss price with a user buyer. You can only lose from this. Price changes expectations of a product. Even if a User knows the price paid, I would still avoid discussing price with them.

    Of course, sometimes the User is also the Economic buyer. In this situation, you have to take the buyer into User buyer mode before discussing prices. Talk about the pain they experience in their work (see tip no 64 – *Avoid Pain*).

Practical Tip No 13

Acknowledge People

This tip mainly applies in retail selling – but not exclusively.

In retail selling, how long do you have to acknowledge someone to give them a good feeling about walking into your store?

One study showed just 1.5 seconds from their crossing the threshold. If you take longer than 1.5 seconds, the best you can hope for is a neutral feeling. If you happened to be away from your desk and get back too late, you will find it harder to approach the prospect. This is about making people feel welcome. If you can do so, then the approach is much easier.

One delegate on a course said to me that was ridiculous, he wasn't acknowledged as he went into the supermarket, within 1.5 seconds. That was precisely my point, how often did he walk into the supermarket and feel 'boy are they pleased to see me in here. They are very welcoming!' In actual fact, in my experience, you are now acknowledged in most supermarkets as you walk in the door. Paco Underhill in his book *'Why We Buy'*, suggested that if it is a little old lady on the door the theft level decreases. You wouldn't steal from a little old lady would you? Look at the door of your local supermarket – is there a security guard at the door, does he or she smile at you?

If you are in a meeting and the door opens, almost everyone will turn around to see who opened it. The same applies in your place of work. You must acknowledge people with a smile, nod of the head, eye contact and so on immediately. If you do this, then when you approach them, you will be more likely to engage them in conversation. The acknowledgement can also take place even when you are dealing with another customer. The chances are the customer you are dealing with will turn to look as well.

What impact does this have if you cannot make eye contact with a shopper entering? Some people try to avoid eye contact. The best you can hope for here is a neutral feeling. They will be the hardest to

87 Practical Tips for Dynamic Selling

approach and you just have to work with that.

I said this applies mainly to retail shopping but not exclusively. I had a meeting with a prospect (now my biggest client) and in reception, I acknowledged and spoke to a lady who was there. I then went into my meeting. During the meeting, the prospect said she wanted to introduce me to her boss and surprise, surprise, it was the lady I had the conversation with. It made the second part much easier.

When coaching salespeople, I constantly remind them of the need to acknowledge people – anyone – it takes no time, it doesn't matter if you acknowledge someone you will never see again, but it will make your job easier occasionally.

It sort of goes hand in hand with the next tip.

Practical Tip No 14

Make Positive Assumptions

I don't like the expression: *'Don't assume, because you make an Ass of U and Me.'*

You must assume. All life is about making assumptions – we must constantly make assumptions. For example, we make assumptions about whether you are a friend or a foe.

I have some advice for you – if you are walking down the street and a couple of guys are walking towards you, wearing balaclavas and carrying Kalashnikov rifles, assume they are terrorists and leg it! They may be going to a fancy dress party but you won't live long if you take these types of risks!

Assume your employer will pay you at the end of the month/week. The only reason your employer pays you is you would rather being doing something else. If your employer stopped paying you would go and do that!

You must make assumptions, of that there is no doubt. The trick in selling is always to make *positive assumptions*. That way Confirmation Bias (see tip no 3) works in your favour.

If you assume everyone will buy from you, then you look for evidence to prove you are right. If you assume your products are the best in the market, then again you seek to prove it. Making positive assumptions is a productive technique.

Assume customers are logical.

Assume customers like you.

Assume if you do your job well, more people will buy from you.

Practical Tip No 15

Approach at the Right Time

You must time your approach to a prospect correctly. I said you must acknowledge immediately – when should you approach? You need to approach people *before the decision has been made* not after.

Retail selling
In retail selling, you must approach when people are on the way in to the showroom, not when they are on the way out! In retail selling, I always recommend an approach as soon as anyone touches something. If prospects touch merchandise, they are evidently looking for some further information and an approach is easy. Give them some of the information they were looking for. *'It opens very easily, doesn't it.' 'It feels very soft, doesn't it.' 'It is very light inside, isn't it.'* etc. I am also making use of tip no 33 – *Getting To 'Yes'* here.

Business to business
In business-to-business, if your approach is after the decision has been made, you are too late. It is always better in these circumstances to find out about their buying process. What have they chosen and what features/benefits does that have that they felt they needed? What did the suppliers do for them that they felt was good?

In business-to-business, you should always find out about budgets and financial years. I have been able to get business and get companies to prepay because they are looking to spend unused budgets. Contact people when the budget is being prepared. Contact them when the financial year is due to end and again as soon as their budgets have been approved.

Of course, you need to contact them at other times as well. We should judge our friends by how they treat us when they don't want something! Customers judge salespeople in the same way. If you only contact them when you need or want something from them, they will quickly tire of your contact. Contacting to give them something useful also uses reciprocation (see tip no 41 – *Reciprocity*).

Practical Tip No 16

Approach in the Right Way

The equivalent to 'Can I help you?' in business-to-business selling is 'How's business?'. Two answers to 'How's business?' seem to recur frequently.

- *'Business is great thanks'* – the implied statement being I am too busy to give you any time and so please hurry up.
- *'Business is really terrible'* – and so I can't afford to pay for whatever you are selling.

Neither of these responses is ideal.

Sometimes these sentiments are expressed even if you don't ask 'How's business'. If these responses are given, you should adopt the attitude that:

1) if business is good, your products will save them time – if they invest a few minutes with you, they can save time and become even more efficient
2) if business is bad, they can spend a few minutes looking at more effective ways of reducing their costs and increasing their profit.

An approach should be surprising, novel or intriguing – it should also be positive. For example, in a retail setting, if you walk up to prospects and say, *'Isn't it amazing?'* in the right tone of voice and then pause, people will ask, *'What is?'*

If you decide to use this approach, my advice would be to think of something amazing first! If you walk up to someone and say, *'Isn't it amazing?'* and they respond, *'What?'*, it isn't very impressive if you then say, *'I don't know – I just read in a book that it was a good thing to say when you approach people'*!

There are some amazing things about showrooms. In the UK, people normally enter, turn left and go round clockwise (because we drive on the left). They will try to avoid other people and so someone sitting or standing can prevent this. If your showroom is set out so that it is difficult to go round clockwise avoiding people, you should reorganise it. We feel more comfortable in an environment that allows us to do this.

People entering a showroom never stop just inside the door. If there is something you want to display although you don't necessarily want people to look for it first – for example brochures – put them immediately inside the door.

I can now hear some people saying to themselves, *'Why would you not want people to look for a brochure?'* This comes from the quaint custom of car dealers who would 'hide' the brochures so that customers would have to talk to a salesperson to get a brochure!

Incidentally, people don't talk to a salesperson nowadays – they simply leave the showroom (never to return!) and check out the product on the Internet.

Back to people not stopping when they enter – it is almost as if people had a landing strip when they enter a showroom. They walk in the door and then their pace decreases until they come to a stop. Most browsers come to a stop at the same distance from the door. This means most people stop at the same display.

An approach could therefore be, *'It's amazing isn't it?'* (pause for a response.) *'What is?'* *'Most people coming in stop to look at this display. Would you mind if I asked you what attracted you to this display?'* You will now find yourself in a conversation. No one will answer, *'No thanks, I am just looking.'*

Evaluative statements

In conversation, evaluative statements are always followed by evaluative statements.

If I make the statement, *'that's a nice colour isn't it'*. People will always tell me what they think of the colour.

87 Practical Tips for Dynamic Selling

Try it out with friends. Start a conversation with 'I think' and see what happens. They will tell you whether they agree or disagree.

It means when approaching someone, you can get in a conversation using evaluative statements.

Of course you now need to work out whether their answer is agreement or disagreement (see tip no 21 – *Agreeing and disagreeing*).

My favourite approach in a showroom is to say, *'The choice is amazing isn't it'*. This works particularly well because most people answer, *'Yes isn't it'*. In using this response, they are implying that they need the guidance of an expert. Luckily for them an expert is usually standing beside them having just uttered the phrase, *'the choice is amazing nowadays isn't it.'!*

In business-to-business selling, the introduction should be something positive. Avoid the weather, the traffic on the way to the appointment and the fish tank in reception. This is because they are the main topics the customer hears from every salesperson and they get bored with it. Try to make it surprising, novel or intriguing and keep it positive.

Practical Tip No 17

Overviews

It is a strange thing about selling but people quickly forget how long it takes them to be comfortable with what is going on.

I think that uncertainty is one of my biggest fears. Remember how it feels being on the outside of an interview room?

To this day, when I am presenting, I have to use some stress reduction techniques just before I am about to present to a large group. It is the waiting and uncertainty that gets to me.

I think when people come in to your place of business, there is a certain amount of fear. Often you can see it in their body language. They don't know what is going to happen to them. Even when I meet someone in their office, there is a certain amount of tension. The same happens in direct selling when you go into someone's home.

One of the roles of the sales person is to reduce the tension. Uncertainty of what is going to happen doesn't help. In particular people don't know two things:

- when they need to make decisions
- when they will start negotiating prices!

In most selling, I have found this to be the case and the salesperson should tackle these fears right up front. A signal that you haven't tackled them is when people ask about discounts before establishing the suitability of the product.

This may be avoided by giving an *overview* of the sales process. The essential component of the overview is to tell people when they need to make decisions and when you will discuss price.

An overview in retail could be:

'The way we normally do business is for you to have a look around the showroom to see if there is anything you like. You don't have to make any decisions at this stage because we can mix and match

87 Practical Tips for Dynamic Selling

anything. When you are ready I will give you some rough prices of the total you could expect to spend including the fitting kits, delivery and the accessories you may have to think about. If you are happy with that then I need you to make some final decisions before I can price everything accurately for you. If you are happy with that who knows you may decide to buy something from me'.

This overview also sets up the use of ball-park figures – see tip no 46.

For an overview in business-to-business selling I use an agenda (see the next tip).

Practical Tip No 18

Agenda

In business-to-business, I use an overview in the form of an agenda. I always use the agenda using these specific words.

'I have been thinking about our meeting and I have prepared an agenda – is there anything you would like to add?'

There is a logic to using these exact words. Let's break the sentence into three parts.

'I have been thinking about our meeting ...'

This phrase should differentiate you from 90% of salespeople. Most go through a meeting demonstrating that they haven't been thinking about the meeting.

'... I have prepared this agenda ...'

Here is some evidence I have been thinking about the meeting.

'... is there anything you would like to add?'

What I have found is that nobody takes anything off the agenda. Some people do add things. Often in my meetings, clients say, *'yes there is another department I want to train'* or *'I would like you to do some follow up on negotiation – could we discuss that too please?'* – and so on.

With only additions likely, this means that you can put a close on the agenda.

For example, a typical agenda for me could be:

87 Practical Tips for Dynamic Selling

Agenda

Meeting 28th January 2005

Attending: Mr Big (Managing Director)   XYZplc
            Mr Next (Financial Director) XYZplc
            David Yule (Principal)   GTi Training

- Background
- Objectives
- Current Skills
- Current Training Needs
- Selling Styles
- Time scale

The final item on the agenda is sometimes as shown here but I do use different ones for other meetings. Others I have used are, *future action* or *next steps*, and I have also used the word *commitment*.

The first time I used 'commitment' when preparing the agenda for a meeting, I thought, 'what if they ask me what I mean by commitment?'

One rule of selling is that, if you might be asked a tricky question, try to think of an answer before you are asked. It is easier to think of a good response when the pressure is off!

I decided that if anyone asked me, I would respond *'that is the commitment we would give you if we were to undertake this contract and what we would need from you in order to provide it'*. In the event no one, so far, has asked.

The real beauty of using an agenda is to remain in control. You should try to stick to the agenda. When something not on the agenda is raised, suggest that you include it in the agenda for the next meeting. This allows you to prepare properly.

64

Practical Tip No 19

We Don't Like to Be Proved Wrong!

Human beings will do almost anything to avoid being proved wrong. I work in Switzerland in the Financial sector, teaching private bankers selling skills. They explained to me the phenomenon of people selling the wrong shares and I explain to them why. Because we don't like to be proved wrong.

One study looked at investment patterns of 10,000 US households and found that investors much preferred to sell off investments that were doing well, i.e. the 'winners' in their portfolio. On the other hand, they were very reluctant to cut their losses and sell off underperforming investments.

Take this scenario
You buy shares in two companies (X & Y). Both companies' shares cost £1 each. Shares in company X go up to £2. Shares in company Y go down and are now worth £0.50. You want to sell one of the shares, which one will you sell? The Swiss private bankers noted that nearly everyone sells the £2 shares. There is no logic to this happening so regularly. There may be special reasons why it makes sense (very occasionally) but not frequently.

Would you sell a company that is well managed, with its shares going up as they are making good profit, and keep shares in a company that appears to be in some trouble, with shares which are sliding?

Often on courses, we have quite a discussion about this. People say you expect company Y shares to increase. Actually, when you bought the shares, you probably expected both to go up so your expectations shouldn't be relied upon! If you look at trends, more companies go out of business following a share slide than following a share hike! If you were buying them for the first time, the shares on the way up look more attractive.

The only logical explanation behind this action is that people don't like to be proved wrong. We sell the £2 share because they make us a profit and that proves we were right to buy them. We hold the £0.50 shares in the hope that they will also increase above £1 and then we can be proved right again!

In selling, this means if you believe anyone is wrong here are some rules.

1. Is it important? If it isn't leave it. If I had been given £1 for every discussion I had heard about someone being wrong even though it was unimportant, I would have, oh, at least a fiver!
2. If it is important, you must make sure they are actually wrong. (see tip no 39 – *Behaviours*) Eagles are never wrong!
3. Get some evidence they are wrong.
4. Get the evidence in writing.
5. Get it before you tell them they are wrong, not after. Saying you think they are wrong and then getting the evidence gives them time to think of a new angle on why they are not wrong!
6. Give them some way to save face, an escape route, e.g. I may have misled you, someone has given you the wrong information, the brochure is misleading, everyone thinks that, it looks that way doesn't it, it must be an optical illusion and so on.

It is hard when selling to prove people wrong and still get the sale. To give yourself the best chance, focus on what is right, not what is wrong. For example, if someone said to me 'this widget doesn't work properly', ask her what she wants it to do rather than ask why it doesn't work.

Practical Tip No 20

Open v Closed Questions

Many years ago I went on a sales training course. The sales trainer said the worst thing in retail selling is that salespeople approach customers and 80% of them say the same words, 'Can I help you?' When you ask this question, over 80% of prospects give the same answer, 'No thanks, I'm just looking'!

The sales trainer said that was because they ask a closed question. He defined a closed question as one that can be answered 'Yes' or 'No'. He said if you ask an open question such as, 'How can I help you?' then people will respond appropriately.

The next day I went up to a prospect in the showroom anxious to try out my new technique. I said 'How can I help you?' The prospect answered, 'You can't thanks, I'm just looking'! Another brilliantly logical technique that doesn't actually work in practice.

People don't answer your questions based on whether it is an open question or not. I have seen many studies on questioning techniques. I have looked at studies defining closed questions in various ways:

A closed question is:
- one that can be answered with a yes or a no, or
- one that encourages a one word answer, or
- one that seeks to get a specific piece of information, facts etc.

An open questions is:
- one that cannot be answered logically with a yes or a no, or
- one that encourages more than a one word answer, or
- one that seeks to get general information about opinions etc.

I have yet to come across any objective study that actually measured success and open questions and has concluded asking more open questions will make you more successful.

I have even seen a study conducted in a call centre on open

67

87 Practical Tips for Dynamic Selling

answers. They measured success and compared it with whether the answers (rather than the questions) were open or closed. They found no correlation between open answers and success.

Imagine a politician being asked a fantastic closed question. 'Were you responsible for this decision?' The likely answer will not involve the words 'yes' or 'no'. In fact, the most likely tactic of the politician is to answer the question they wanted you to ask them, rather than the one you did!

Imagine a burglar who robbed a bank last Thursday. The police arrest him. To digress for just a minute, I have some advice for would-be criminals. If the police arrest you, try not to help them with their enquiries. In fact try to be as obstructive as possible with their enquiries. I have noticed a very strong correlation between people that 'help the police with their enquiries' and those subsequently being charged with the offence!

Anyway this burglar is sitting in the interview room. Imagine the scene – there is a strong light shining directly into the robber's face, the room is quite dark and dingy. The robber is tense. The detective asks, 'What were you doing at 3pm on Thursday?' The robber answers, 'Fair cop, guv! Too good a question for me. If only you had asked a closed question, I'd've got away wiv it!'

People don't answer your questions based on whether it is a great question or not. They answer it based on whether they trust you and want to give you the information. That is why in selling you should focus on developing rapport with prospects rather than on your questioning style.

Someone recently told me they have improved their success by asking, 'How do you take your tea?' rather than, 'Would you like a cup of tea?' Good luck with this and if it works for you keep doing it. Personally I might be inclined to respond with 'Why do you ask!' rather than tell you I take milk and just a little sugar!

My tip is to forget about whether you are asking open or closed questions. Look at tip no 23 – *Understanding and Selling questions* and tip no 25 – *Secondary Questioning*

Practical Tip No 21

Agreeing and Disagreeing

I think the idea of open and closed questions came about because salespeople ignored what they knew. When we ask a closed question we sometimes take disagreement as agreement. We do this even when we know it is not the case.

There are clear differences between agreement and disagreement even when people seem to be using the same language.

Start with the statement, *'That's a nice colour, isn't it.'* Of the following answers, one is agreement and the other disagreement.

'Yes, it is really lovely, isn't it.' (responded to quickly without a pause).
(Pause) *'Yeees, it's okay, isn't it.'*

Both appear to be agreeing but they are not.

When people are agreeing with you, they respond immediately without a pause. They also upgrade what you say. In the example above, 'nice' was upgraded to 'really lovely'.

When people disagree they pause before replying. Then they downgrade what you said. In the example 'nice' was downgraded to 'okay'.

I think we know this without being told. Some salespeople ask a closed question, get an answer that they know isn't really an agreement but plough on regardless.

The example I used in trial closes (tip no 11) was *'Do you think this would suit you?'* By the language and pause, you will be able to tell whether it does or doesn't. Don't take a positive answer at face value – follow your instincts. If necessary, this may be a good time to create an objection (tip no 83) and use some consistency (tip no 50), e.g. *'You don't sound very certain, why do you think it is suitable for you?'*

Practical Tip No 22

Waiting

Perception of reading and time
When we read, our perception of time changes. In a queue of people, some are reading and some aren't. The people in the queue who are reading estimate on average that they have been waiting for less time than the people who are not reading.

Not seeing a clock also changes perception of time. This is why your dentist's waiting room will probably have old magazines and probably not have a clock!!

Music
Research has shown that music can be used to help create the image of your business and to increase sales.

Attracting and prolonging customer visits
'The Draw of Live Music', a study conducted by Dr Adrian North from the University of Leicester in 2003, showed that:

'Live music is a social event – it particularly attracts couples, friends and party groups. In the study, 93% of the audience came in parties of 2 or more.'

In another study by North & Hargreaves (1999), music increased the amount of time customers spent waiting in a retail shop. Three different types of music were played but the same result was obtained with each type of music.

In a 'telephone hold' experiment, the time spent holding only increased when the music was liked by the caller.

Music should therefore be chosen based on the typical caller. This is probably why, if you are holding for 'Virgin Mobile', you can choose your music.

There is a link between the tempo of the music and the speed people walk at. Customers walk more slowly with slow music and

87 Practical Tips for Dynamic Selling

faster with fast music. Since your objective in retail should be to prolong the time spent in store you should have slow music playing. In an experiment (Milliman in 1982), they also spent more money when slow music was playing!

The genre of music being played affects the perception of your business. For example, when classical music is playing, surveys report a sophisticated perception. When pop music was playing the perception was upbeat and lively.

A study investigated how stereotypical French and German music can influence the selection of French and German wines. Over a two week period, French and German music was played on alternate days at an in-store display of evenly priced wines. French music led to French wines outselling German wines 3:1 and the German music led to the German wines outselling the French wines 2:1. When customers were questioned leaving the store, they were unaware of any effects and denied any influence from the music.

This study also showed that when classical music was played, the average spend per bottle of wine increased. More worryingly, when the wrong type of music was played, customers spent less and became more aggressive – one customer even threatening violence if the music wasn't switched off!

Classical music played in a British restaurant increased the spend on starters, coffee, total spend on food and overall spend. It wasn't reported whether there were significant differences on the amount spent on main courses, desserts or overall drinks bill even though these were measured.

If you use music in your business, you may have to experiment with the type of music and volume. This may not apply to a field salesperson but could also still be used should the customer visit your place of business.

When anyone is doing nothing – give them something to read. This applies even in field sales. If you are working on something, for example, working out figures, give the customer something to read.

Practical Tip No 23

Understanding and Selling Questions

Questions asked by a salesperson come from two different directions. They can either be questions that help the salesperson to sell or questions which help them to understand the needs of the prospect.

I do an exercise on courses to illustrate this.

I find someone in the audience who has a fear of something. Let's say I have a volunteer who has a fear of water. I will refer to this volunteer as the 'Fear Volunteer'.

I ask him to sit out in the middle of the room.

I then ask for a volunteer who loves scuba diving. I ask him what his hobbies are and what is a perfect weekend for him. I will refer to this volunteer as the 'Selling Volunteer'.

We now have a 'fear volunteer' who has a fear of water. Another who loves football and diving, and a perfect weekend would be to watch the UEFA cup final in Rome.

I offer an all expenses paid trip for the 'selling volunteer' and a partner of their choice, to the UEFA cup final which is next Wednesday. I check they are free to fly out on Wednesday and back Thursday or Friday. They usually are! I also offer £200 spending money.

All that they have to do to earn this fabulous trip is to get the other person on a diving trip this weekend. I have organised a boat and it leaves at 2 o'clock on Sunday. Can they persuade them to come on the trip?

Both participants have heard the briefing. They both know what each other is likely to do.

I will relate the typical approach.

87 Practical Tips for Dynamic Selling

Sales Volunteer:	What are you doing on Sunday?
Fear Volunteer:	I am busy visiting friends!
SV:	We have something fabulous lined up that I am sure you will enjoy. How would you like to come with us?
FV:	What is it?
SV:	Well it is a life-changing experience that you will really enjoy.
FV:	Is it dangerous?
SV:	No, no it is perfectly safe.
FV:	What do I have to do?
SV:	Nothing – you just have to come out with us and enjoy the day?
FV:	When you say out what do you mean?
SV:	Do you like boats?
FV:	Yes, I don't mind boats provided they are quite big and it is not too rough and I don't need to go near water.
SV:	Oh no, this boat is very big and I am sure it won't be rough on Sunday. I have checked the weather forecast and it is really good.
FV:	Okay, then I might come with you.
SV:	Have you ever wondered what it was like under the sea? The beautiful sights and the lovely fish. Do you like fish?
FV:	Only on a plate!
SV:	Underwater is really beautiful.
FV:	Yes but I don't like water.
SV:	Why is that?
FV:	I am just frightened of it. I get cold sweats when I think of it. I think …
SV:	Have you ever thought of confronting your fear?
FV:	I have tried many times and every time it fails.
SV:	Why has it failed?
FV:	I am frightened I am going to drown.
SV:	So, if I could get it really safe and in fact if the boat didn't go out very far. In fact you don't even need to go out of your depth do you? (They then ask me – 'you

87 Practical Tips for Dynamic Selling

	didn't say they had to be out of their depth did you?' I respond it is not a condition to be out of their depth)
FV:	No I don't think so. What's in it for me?
SV:	Well you get an opportunity to overcome your fear. Do you like football?
FV:	Yes I do, why?
SV:	If you did this you could come with me to see the UEFA cup final.
FV:	No thanks.
SV:	What if I gave you £100 spending money and all expenses paid?
FV:	No I'm not interested.

The strategy that the 'sales volunteer' followed here is the strategy I think people naturally follow to sell something if they haven't been trained to sell. Let me break it down.

Step No 1

They go for a close at the beginning.

Sales volunteer   What are you doing on Sunday?

This is a failure strategy. The suspicion and distrust that is built up here makes it very difficult to sell. The equivalent in selling is to ask:

'Are you the buyer, Managing Director, responsible for making the buying decision etc?'

'Do you use .... Product?
'Are you interested in saving money?'   These are typical
'What is your budget?'   'qualification'
'When are you looking to buy?'   questions

If you ask questions like these, don't be surprised if people don't tell you the truth. If someone doesn't tell you the truth, then to me it is self-evident they don't trust you.

One of the ways to identify selling questions is that people often do not tell the truth when answering. That is where we get the expression, 'buyers are liars'. It isn't because people are inherent

87 Practical Tips for Dynamic Selling

liars. If you ask a question that people would be stupid to answer with the truth, then expect them to lie.

Step No 2
They ignore objections early on:

Fear Volunteer:	I am busy visiting friends!
S:	We have something fabulous lined up that I am sure you will enjoy. How would you like to come with us?
FV:	What is it?
S:	Well it is a life-changing experience that you will really enjoy.

Step No 3
They get asked a difficult question and they answer with a lie! Either that or they hide the real purpose – one reason there is a trend towards consultants and designers rather than salespeople.

FV:	Is it dangerous?
SV:	No, no it is perfectly safe.
FV:	What do I have to do?
SV:	Nothing – you just have to come out with us and enjoy the day?

Step No 4
They 'sell the benefits':

SV:	Have you ever wondered what it was like under the sea? The beautiful sights and the lovely fish. Do you like fish?
FV:	Only on a plate!
SV:	Underwater is really beautiful.

Step No 5
They ask 'why' at all the wrong times (see tip no 6 – *When to avoid the most powerful word in selling*).

FV:	Yes but I don't like water.
SV:	Why is that?

87 Practical Tips for Dynamic Selling

Step No 6
They miss information by interrupting.

FV:	I am just frightened of it. I get cold sweats when I think of it. I think…….
SV:	Have you ever thought of confronting your fear?
FV:	I have tried many times and every time it fails.

Step No 7
They miss buying signals and don't use 'why?' at the right times. The right question now would be, 'Why have you tried to confront your fear?'.

SV:	Why has it failed?
FV:	I am frightened I am going to drown.

Step No 8
Then they go back to closing using the, 'If I could, then would you?' close.

SV:	So if I could get it really safe and in fact if the boat didn't go out very far … in fact you don't even need to go out of your depth do you?

Step No 9
And finally we get to bribery. It isn't that the 'fear volunteer' was price sensitive. The 'selling volunteer' encouraged them to be price sensitive because of their selling strategy.

FV:	No I don't think so. What's in it for me?
SV:	Well, you get an opportunity to overcome your fear. Do you like football?
FV:	Yes I do, why?
SV:	If you did this, you could come with me to see the UEFA cup final.

Using this approach, I think that a negotiation is an inevitable consequence of the strategy. Human beings all listen to the same radio station. It is called WIIFM (What's in it for me?). If you try to get someone to buy from you because it is what you need, then negotiation is an inevitable consequence.

It is helpful to consider here that people don't generally know what they need. The salesperson must help them to understand what they need and want. If you ask a direct question, the answer will not be useful. For example 'How important is delivery to you?' The answer may be, 'very important', but that does not help the prospect place a value on that need. To do so you need to ask *understanding* questions to help them.

Returning to the exercise, usually the 'fear volunteer' is a little stressed at this stage. They normally want to speak about the fear and the 'selling volunteer' has prevented this from happening.

It takes me a little while to calm them down. I usually talk a little of my fear as well. I don't like being out of my depth in water when I can't see what else is in the water. I don't mind swimming pools but Liverpool Docks holds no attraction for me!

I then ask them about their fear. I have had some hairy stories on courses about people nearly drowning, being pushed into harbours before they could swim, so-called 'friends' terrifying the living daylights out of them. Often on the course, the other delegates (that have until now been solely observers) start to get interested in the story and asking understanding questions.

I would like to keep them talking as long as I can, exploring next their feelings about what happened to them. I ask them about other situations – holidays and so on. I ask them about friends and family. Do their children swim? How do they feel about that?

Then I will look at the buying signal. *'You said you had tried many times to conquer it – why have you tried many times?'* This is the correct use of 'why' It is a positive situation, I want them to try again and so I always ask why (see tip no 7 – *When to use the most powerful word in selling*).

They will now tell me that they are desperate to overcome their fear. They have tried many times because they see others enjoying themselves and they feel left out.

I then introduce a solution. I had a friend that was frightened of water and they went to an NLP practitioner (see tip no 31 – *NLP*). I believe NLP is good for phobias and fears. The practitioner took them through a thought process without even going near water. After one hour, the NLP practitioner ask what my friend wanted to happen next. They said they were going straight to a swimming pool to jump in the water which they did. Everybody lived happily ever after.

Does the prospect want me to introduce them to the NLP practitioner? Often they say yes. Oh, one other thing, the NLP practitioner does make a charge – are they willing to pay? I have had people agreeing to pay substantial sums of money if they could have various fears removed. Why wouldn't they pay?

In this way, I can help someone's problems and get them to pay for it. I am not teaching them to be price sensitive, I am teaching them the value of the solution. Any negotiation is based on how much extra they are prepared to pay rather than how much I have to bribe them with.

Of course, fairy tales are easy in books. Sometimes the approach fails. Some people are happy with their fear and are desperate to hold on to it. In these cases, we don't make a sale. My contention here is that my job is not to get a sale at any cost. That is short-term thinking. My job is simply to see if what I sell would be a beneficial purchase for the prospect. Do they need it and if so how much is it worth to them?

The process I use here is a completely different mind-shift away from selling towards understanding people. When I understand prospects, I discover if what I am selling is of any value to them.

It is as simple as that. What you are selling is a by-product. If it happens to meet with the needs of your prospect, you get a sale. If your product does not meet with the needs of your prospect, you don't get a sale – and nor should you! If you get a sale in these circumstances, you have either misled your customer or misunderstood them. Either way you cannot get repeat business on this basis.

Some characteristics of *selling* and *understanding* questions

Selling Questions

- Selling questions are leading, e.g. *'What do you think of the service you are getting from your current supplier?'*

- You have a solution you have thought of before asking the question, e.g. *'Were you happy with the response rate to your campaign?'* The example is for a data supplier for marketing campaigns. Your thought process being if you weren't happy, the solution is to buy our product!
- There is a perfect answer as far as you are concerned, e.g. *'What is your budget?'*
- Clients don't always answer truthfully, e.g. all of the above!
- The answer is only for your benefit and so the customer wouldn't lose anything if the question were never asked, e.g. *'Have you had any other quotations?'*
- They are fact finding, e.g. *'What is your buying level of authority?'*
- They are commitment based, e.g. *'If there was a product that did this for you, would you buy it?'*

Understanding Questions

- Although the question may be about the past, the reason you are asking is to help future decisions, e.g. *'What do you like about your existing product?'*
- They are about the clients values/beliefs/opinions, e.g. *'What would be the three most important things for you to achieve in the next financial year?'*
- They address any concerns the client may have, e.g. *'What would you see as the biggest obstacle to a successful product launch?'*
- Clients almost always answer truthfully
- They are asked only for the benefit of the client to make sure that no mistakes are made in suggesting the wrong product or service.
- There is no commitment to buy implied by answering the question
- They are 'nice to know' questions rather than need to know questions.

Note

The distinction between the types of questions is not clear-cut. The determining factor being whether the question is being asked because it helps you to sell or are you are asking it to determine the right product for the client.

This is why there is not a clear distinction, because selecting the right product obviously makes it easier to sell.

If there is any doubt in the client's mind, they sometimes ask, *'Why do you want to know that?'* To avoid this if there is any doubt, then explain your reason for asking the question before asking it.

Practical Tip No 24

Take Notes

For me, too much is made of questioning skills on sales training courses and not enough made of taking notes. I was reading a Selling Skills book where the author said you should ask for permission before taking notes. This must be an American thing. I have never had anyone object to my taking notes and indeed it is expected in many cases. Not taking notes is a bigger problem!

Would you trust a salesperson that tried to commit everything to memory? Would you trust a doctor that didn't have a filing system and said they never refer to patient notes? *'Just call me. I remember every patient's prescriptions.'* Oh, yeah?

There are a few benefits to taking notes (any notes – it doesn't even matter the quality!)

- First of all, people slow down when you are taking notes so that you get everything down.
- Second, people are more truthful when you are writing things down! I think this is because there is a record of what they said and so they stick more closely to the truth.
- Third, you appear to be professional and interested in the longer term.
- Fourth, it helps you to use silence because when you are writing you don't need to speak.

If you can take good notes, then so much the better.

One tip when taking notes – review them as soon as possible after and write clarifying notes for those you may not understand in the near future. Have you ever come across notes of a meeting you had a few years earlier. Boy, is it hard to remember what your own notes mean!

Practical Tip No 25

Secondary Questioning

Secondary questioning is asking a question about the previous answer rather than thinking of a new question.

Have you ever been with a prospect and you couldn't think of a question to ask? That is probably because you are thinking of new questions on new subjects!

Imagine you get a very small piece of information from me; I play golf. If you use secondary questioning, there are lots of questions you could now ask.

'Where do I play?'
'How often?'
'Who do I play with?'
'What is my handicap?'
'What is my best score?'
... and so on.

When selling there are times when you are fact-finding. This is when you need fewer interactions and more information. During fact finding, all good salespeople use secondary questioning.

You might notice that secondary questioning combined with the one-second rule (see tip no 29) makes open and closed questions irrelevant to all intents and purposes.

Suppose you ask someone a closed question, e.*g*. *'Does it cause you problems when the goods are delivered late?'*

First of all, using the one-second rule (see tip no 29) will mean people will never only answer yes or no to this question. With the one-second rule, a typical answer would be something like:

'Yes, it causes us big problems ... .because we can't then deliver on time to our customers ... and that hurts our reputation,' or *'No, it doesn't cause us problems ... what we do is we build in a margin*

87 Practical Tips for Dynamic Selling

because we know that deliveries come late and so we tell our customers that it takes 2-3 weeks ... and they have usually delivered within that time ... that's how we get round it anyway.'

If you don't use the one-second rule and instead use secondary questioning, the typical conversation may sound something like:

'Does it cause you problems when the goods are delivered late?'
'Yes.'
'What happens?'
'Well we have told our customers that delivery will take 2-3 weeks and we have to telephone them.'
'Are they accommodating?'
... and so on

Alternatively of course, the answer can be in the negative, i.e.
'Does it cause you problems when the goods are delivered late?'
'No.'

This was always the big argument for using open questions. I think you get the same answer if you ask:

'What problems does it cause you when the goods are delivered late?'
'None!'

With these answers, the best strategy is understanding questions, the one second rule and then secondary questioning. To help with secondary questioning, you can look for *Key Words and Clue Words* – see Tip no 26, next.

Practical Tip No 26

Key Words and Clue Words

Key Words

In virtually every sentence there is a **key word**. Consider the following sentence:

'We are looking for quick deliveries.'

The key word here is 'quick' and you now need to ask secondary questions to find out:

'What does 'quick' mean to you?'

'What impact does it have on your business when it is 'quick' and what impact when it is slow?'

Another example:

'Well, we have told our customers that delivery will take 2-3 weeks and we have to telephone them.'

Here 'customers', 'deliver' and 'telephone' are the key words and the questions that follow should be around these.

Focus your secondary questions around key words. With a little practice you will find it happening automatically.

Clue Words

Another thing that I look for to give me opportunities are **clue words**.

These are words such as: *usually, normally, prefer* and *sometimes*.

For example a prospect may say: *'Our existing suppliers are normally very good with deliveries.'*

You must pick up the clue word and question around that.

'You mentioned they normally are good what happens when they are late?'

Another example:

'We would prefer to get deliveries in the morning.'

Here 'morning' is the key word and 'prefer' is the clue word. You would then follow up with secondary questions about the morning and about their preferences.

Practical Tip No 27

Budgets

My tip is never to ask a potential customer for their budget. If you really want to do so, wait until you have developed a great deal of trust. I know this tip is fairly controversial since many excellent salespeople ask for a budget. Let me state my case.

First of all when you ask for a budget, not many people tell you. The ones that do tell you often don't tell you truthfully. The ones that tell you truthfully almost always spend more than they anticipated.

The fact is that most people don't tell the truth (some consciously some subconsciously), and I don't blame them – neither would I, if I were asked this question!

Therefore, the reason you are asking for a budget must be for reasons other than to find out how much money people will spend.

There are some compelling reasons for *not* asking for a budget.

Imagine you went into a doctor's surgery and the doctor talked about an operation and then asked you how much you could afford to spend. How much trust would you place in this doctor? There is no surer way to make it difficult to build trust than to ask for a budget.

You are ignoring the way people shop. If we decide to buy a carpet for our house, the conversation doesn't go like this:

Me: Good morning dear, what would you like to do today?
Wife: I would like to buy a new carpet.
Me: How much shall we spend?
Wife: We can only afford to spend £1000!
Me: 'Maybe we should go to the bank then to arrange a loan in case we need to spend more than this!

More typically, people don't actually have any idea how much things cost until they go and start to look. Budgets aren't decided, they are formed.

Asking people to enunciate a budget means that when they have

87 Practical Tips for Dynamic Selling

told you a figure, you have created a mental barrier for them that you now have to overcome (in most cases). Because we don't like to be proved wrong (tip no 19), you have actually made the sale more difficult for yourself.

Because of comparison theory (tip no 58) you have, in all probability, made the price seem higher than if you had used price conditioning rather than asking about budgets.

In any event there are better ways of going about it. (see tip no 60 – *Top Down Selling*)

Practical Tip No 28

Cialdini

Read the book *'Influence – The Science and Practice'* by Robert Cialdini!

ISBN 0-321-01147-3, Published by Allyn & Bacon

Practical Tip No 29

The One-second Rule

As children, we are taught by parents to take our turn in conversations. You can see evidence in children as young as three months old taking turns. What happens is that mummy says, 'goo goo ga ga', and waits, then baby says, 'goo goo ga ga'. Babies may say 'ga ga goo goo' rather than 'goo goo ga ga' for all I know!

What this means is that in any conversation, if I signal it is still your turn to speak, you will carry on. The most important signal that it is still your turn is a pause of about one second. The impact of turn taking is that, in any conversation, if there is a gap of less than one second, someone will fill it!

Here is another sign of turn taking. When someone doesn't want it to be your turn they make noises such as 'Emmm'. Another way is to use 'nothing' words. You know the words, you know, I mean, you know. I am told, you know, that footballers, you know, especially David Beckham, you know, are particularly, you know, good at, I mean, using them. I apologise to Mr Beckham for impersonating him and leaving out so many 'you knows' but I couldn't even stand writing them – far less listening to them!

If I am speaking with someone and they appear to have come to the end, I leave one second, invariably they go on to say almost the same thing a different way. Another second gap and they will add a little more information. If I use it too often, people will start then to answer their own questions. Another one second gap and they say 'well that's what I think anyway.' One second later and they are feeling the pressure but still they go on to say, 'because ...'

I demonstrate this on courses. Someone on a course will ask my opinion or ask a question and I use the one-second rule. Usually the first few times I use this technique the audience doesn't notice its use. This is even though I have explained it and told them I will use it to demonstrate. On day two, some of the audience notice. The person

87 Practical Tips for Dynamic Selling

speaking who is subjected to the one-second rule never notices.

I have a theory here. I don't think it is possible to train people out of a behaviour. Suppose you put up a sign saying 'Wet Paint' on a fence and observe the behaviour of passers by. For 20 years, they have passed the fence without feeling the need to touch it, but now? They just have to touch it to see if it is still wet.

Ask any waitress what happens when they say to diners, *'Please be careful – the plate is hot'*. Somehow people are compelled to check.

In the UK, I think a massive problem has been created by this phenomenon. The government have been trying to say to young people, 'Don't take drugs'. I don't know if you have noticed, but since these campaigns, drug taking has boomed.

Malcolm Gladwell in his book *'The Tipping Point'* claimed that drugs are not particularly physically addictive. Trying a drug once doesn't get most people physically addicted. Addiction can of course be mental or physical. It is what he calls the 'stickiness' of drugs that get people hooked. His researched showed that less than 0.9% of people (that is 9 people in 1000) who try heroine get addicted to it. It isn't the testing of it that is addictive. If drugs could get you physically addicted by just trying them there would be many more addicts. I am told that the vast majority of people under 30 have tried drugs.

Cocaine certainly isn't particularly addictive. Less than 0.3% of people who try cocaine get addicted to it. When I was young, in the UK if you went to the dentist to have a tooth extracted they offered the option of gas or an injection to anaesthetise the area. They didn't use the word 'injection' they said, *'Do you want gas or cocaine?'* I have never heard of anyone going back to a dentist and asking for another injection because they were hooked!

I say this because I have noticed some salespeople interrupt the customer too often. When coaching, I have tried many times to get a salesperson to interrupt less and listen more. Asking people to focus on not doing something, like interrupting, is an unsuccessful approach. Don't think of a desert island at the moment with blue sea, and palm trees waving in the wind!

If you don't want your children to take drugs don't tell them not to try them. You might try the *Absolutely Fabulous* method. In this television programme, the mother (Jennifer Saunders) acts like the teenager whilst the daughter, Saffie (Julia Sawalha) acts like the disappointed parent. Saffie wouldn't take drugs. Children try to avoid the mistakes their parents made.

Instead of focusing on interrupting less, try focussing on using the one-second rule more.

In particular, one time that you need to focus on the one-second rule is when closing. I define closing as asking the customer for some commitment or for some future action. So a close could be, *'Shall we schedule a meeting to discuss this further?'* or *'Do you want me to order it now for you?'*

When asking people to buy, it is said (and I agree) that the first person that speaks own it!

If you ask for any future action (remembering to use 'because' – see tip no 8) you must use silence after you have made the request until the other person speaks. This applies even if you remember the most compelling reason for the action which you forgot to bring out. If you start up again with the compelling reason, you will find the discussion moving to the compelling reason rather than the action.

Don't speak after closing!

Practical Tip No 30

Go for Small Orders

Every salesman I have ever employed has thought about getting the really big order. I presume they feel that if they get a really big order on January the 1st, they will be able to put up their feet and rest for the remainder of the year.

I have news for them. If you get a massive piece of business on January the first, your target will increase on January 2nd!! No employer would let you cruise for a year. Perhaps the best day to get a massive piece of business would be on 24th December so you make your target and enjoy Christmas!

From a business perspective, small pieces of business are much better. Having many different customers means that you are not as vulnerable as having only one client.

Big pieces of business tend to be more competitive with smaller margins.

I once worked with the fifth largest (at that time) electronic component distributor in the world. We regularly made more profit than the top four put together. Sure they had big turnover but they went for the competitive OEM (original equipment manufacturers) business. They worked on very small margins. We looked for the maintenance and repair market. If you are looking for a semiconductor or a relay to fix equipment, you are more concerned with being able to find it than what price it is. Our margins were huge.

Most big companies consider the 'Pareto' principle at some time.

Pareto was an Italian economist and political philosopher. He showed that 20% of the nation owned 80% of the wealth. This has been further developed as Pareto's law which has also become known as the 80/20 rule. The 80/20 rule appears to apply to almost anything. 80% of your customers produce 20% of your profit. Conversely 20% of your customers use up 80% of your resources.

If 80% of customers produce only 20% of the profit, most

87 Practical Tips for Dynamic Selling

companies reason that they could get rid of at least 5% of their customers and lose nothing. They ignore that it is easier to retain business than it is to get new business. They also ignore that oak trees grow from acorns.

Surely, rather than getting rid of customers, you should follow tip no 55 – *Never Say No*. Try to make more money from them so that they contribute more to the profit. Put the prices up! You would be amazed how many customers will stay with you.

When I was running a training course in Switzerland, one of the bankers told a story. His bank had decided to start charging for some services they had included for free. I asked what percentage of people stopped buying? Around 2% I was told. When they embarked on the exercise, they originally decided they would just stop offering the service because they felt people wouldn't pay for it. In the event almost everyone did.

I suggest you look for small business and find a way of making big profit from it.

Small business is less price sensitive and so you avoid teaching customers to be price sensitive. Teaching customers to be price sensitive is quite common. When companies take on a new piece of business, many focus on price reductions or at least better quality for the same price. We teach customers who are not price sensitive to be so by the way we sell.

It is easier to monitor a small piece of business and make sure the service is excellent. It is easier to screw up a big first order!

It doesn't make sense and is inconsistent to give a small piece of business to someone you would not do more with. By getting the small piece first, you make it easier to get a big chunk. This is using the consistency rule (see tip no 50)

When you use the 'Spare Tyre' contact strategy (see tip no 40) you should always be trying for a little order. There are several advantages. Prospects feel under pressure to give you some business if you follow up well. If it a small piece of business they, and competitors, may feel it is insignificant. It is not.

Practical Tip No 31

NLP (Neuro-Linguistic Programming)

I am not a huge fan of NLP although I would recommend that you should read a book on it. If you get more than me, good luck. NLP is the brainchild of Richard Bandler and John Grinder.

What I have found useful from NLP is the concept that people think in three modes – Visual, Auditory and Kinaesthetic. I prefer to call kinaesthetic Tactile, (mainly because the first time I came across it I had to look it up in a dictionary!)

That is a rather silly statement because the first time I came across 'tactile' I had to find our what it meant as well. It is rather like when someone says, 'it is always in the last place you look, isn't it'. You would hardly be looking for something, find it and say, 'I must keep on looking so that it isn't in the last place I look!!'

Anyway, people operate in three modes, Visual, Auditory and Tactile.

Because it is NL (linguistic) P, you get a clue as to which mode someone is in from their language. You may also get clues from eye movements. Looking up is more visual, looking down more tactile and looking at eye level more auditory.

People operating in a visual mode say things like:

'I can _see_ what you mean but it _looks_ like we would have difficulty with that in our organisation.'

People operating in an auditory mode would say for the same statement:

'I can _hear_ what you say but it _sounds_ like we would have difficulty with that in our organisation.'

And in a tactile mode, people would say:

'I _feel_ very uncomfortable with that, it would be very _hard_ to do in our organisation.'

Bandler and Grinder think that we develop rapport with people very quickly when they operate in the same mode as us. We also find it very hard to develop rapport with people who operate in other modes.

I haven't found this to be particularly useful. I am not saying it doesn't work – I just haven't put in the effort that I need to in order to determine what mode other people are operating in.

What I have found to be very useful is that, when I have made a mistake, it hits me right between the eyes. I find it very easy to see which mode to answer in.

For example, suppose someone says to me:

'I don't see what you mean,' or, *'It doesn't sound useful for us,'* or *'That would be hard to get accepted,'* then I can pick up the mode very quickly. In essence, I use it reactively rather than proactively. I don't use it to develop rapport, I prefer to try to develop rapport naturally. If you are interested, see Dale Carnegie's book *How to Win Friends and Influence People*. It describes great ways to build rapport.

Practical Tip No 32

Sell to the Woman, Close to the Man

I can hear the political correctness screams already.

I have no moral conscience in this – I am only taking my personal experience and my own observations.

In my experience, the woman makes the decision on what to buy for anything that will be inside the home. We recently bought a television for the study. Even though I will undoubtedly watch this particular television more than my wife, she decided which one. Sure I was consulted, I could have vetoed a set but the final choice had to be decided by my wife.

My wife tends to buy for aesthetic reasons, it has to look nice. I buy for practical reasons, it has to function well. Because the look of our home is more important to my wife she (rightly) has to have the final decision over anything inside.

Now, if we are buying a barbecue, a lawnmower, a car or whatever, I have the final decision on these. Anything that goes outside the house, I usually have the final decision. I think this happened even with her car. She looked to me for advice and confirmation and so I had the final word even if it was only 'yes dear!'

It may not be politically correct, but if what you are selling is to be used inside the home, try to support the woman's argument. If it is used outside, try to support the man.

To support a woman's argument, no man in his right mind will buy something that is harder to keep clean! If you say the man's choice is harder to keep clean, the man will visibly crumble!

To support a man's argument, imply that the alternatives take more time. Women tend to want things that will save the man time so that he can spend more time with her.

87 Practical Tips for Dynamic Selling

Stand in a supermarket or observe people in a restaurant. When a couple are about to pay, whose credit card or cash is used? In my experience, it is the man that pays the vast majority of the time.

When I say 'pays', I mean the action rather than the money actually coming from his pocket. I don't want to get into any more trouble than I already am! I was hoping that the occasional female might read my book!

For some reason, men take a perverse pleasure out of paying. I think this is from conditioning that we must be the providers. For that reason, I think this is changing and younger people are acting differently.

More young men get involved in the decision to buy things in the home. Younger women pay more often in restaurants and supermarkets.

The good news is that if you disagree with this tip it is probably because you are much younger than me!!

If men take pleasure out of paying, sell to the woman and close to the man.

Practical Tip No 33

Getting to 'Yes'

To get someone to answer 'yes' to your question, you should phrase your question using a positive followed by a negative.

It doesn't work one hundred percent of the time but almost!

'That is *(+ tive)* a nice colour isn't *(– tive)* it?' – will almost always be answered starting with 'yes'.

The opposite works too:

'That isn't *(– tive)* a nice colour, is *(+ tive)* it?' – will almost always be answered starting with 'no'.

This is especially important when closing, e.g. 'So you would like me to place the order now, wouldn't you,' is better than the opposite.

A word on tone here – this has to be said as a statement rather than a question. In the UK, we signify a question by going up in tone at the end of the sentence. To use this effectively, you must go down in tone at the end.

If you find it difficult to phrase in a positive then negative way when closing it may be because you are closing too early. It can also be an indication that you are not asking enough trial closes (see tip no 11 – *Think*) during the sale.

Practical Tip No 34

'Three Yes' Technique

This is a technique that has been taught to many sales staff and has been abused to the extent it now annoys people. It isn't the techniques itself that annoys people, it is the poor use of it.

I am sure you have heard the 'three yes' technique. You are at home enjoying a lovely evening meal. The phone rings. When you answer it the conversation goes something like:

Caller: 'Is that David Yule?'
Me: 'Yes, who's ...?'
Caller: 'Do you live at ----?'
Me: 'What are you selling?'
Caller: 'Are you interested in saving mon ... click – rrrrrrrrrrrrrrrrr'

That was poor use of the three yes technique!

The idea of the technique is that we develop rapport with people who answer yes three times to our first three *evaluative* statements! Poor use is when we ask three stupid rhetorical questions that annoy the living daylights out of people!

When you meet someone at a party and you say, 'The government has handled that crisis well!' and they agree with you – that is the first 'yes'. Then you say, 'Did you watch that programme last night?' and they say, 'Yes, I did it was excellent, wasn't it' – that is your second 'yes'.

Next you say, 'I felt sorry for the main character, I think he should have been released,' and they say, 'You know, I think exactly the same. That was a complete injustice wasn't it?' That is your third 'yes' and you now have developed complete rapport with this stranger. They think like you and they agree with you. You have started a possible friendship well.

The trouble with this technique for sales is that it is a risky

87 Practical Tips for Dynamic Selling

strategy. If you say, 'The government has handled that crisis well,' and they disagree with you, that is the first 'no'. Then you say, 'Did you watch that programme last night?' They say, 'No, I don't watch that type of thing, but I heard about it.' That is your second 'no'.

Next you say, 'I felt sorry for the main character, I think he should have been released,' and they say, 'You know, I think we are completely soft on these rogues – we need to take a harder line, capital punishment for shoplifting is my view!' You may as well cut your losses and go speak to someone else! You have started a possible friendship but with someone else at the party!

The reason I have shown this as a tip is that I found many salespeople staring meetings with prospects asking questions that were almost guaranteed 'no' answers.

Watch your questions, particularly at the beginning. Do you ask 'yes' questions or 'no' questions?

Practical Tip No 35

Two Brochures

Whenever you are reading something to a customer, or looking up something in a brochure, if at all possible get two brochures. Give one to the customer and have one yourself.

Have you ever stood feeling like a dummy when someone is looking for something in a brochure. I have even been standing thinking to myself, if you just let me have one, I know where to find what you are looking for.

I like salespeople to be experts in the products. That is the added value of a salesperson for me personally. I actually avoid salespeople who are over-friendly. Give me a product expert any day.

What I really don't like is when I ask the salesperson a question and they start to read the box. Now you are wasting my time. I have just read the box! I know you think most customers are idiots but I don't think I am! I wish they would ask me if there is anything on the box about the product and listen to my answer. If they then have to go and look for some back up material, say a brochure or manual, I would like them to give a brochure to me as well and I will help.

It stops me from feeling useless and gives me something to do. That keeps the sales opportunity going for longer and there is a strong correlation between time and selling. (see tip no 36 – *Correlations*)

Practical Tip No 36

Correlations

Time

There is a strong correlation between time and buying (longer time in a shop means more buying). In fact, I was working with a group of direct salespeople who felt the correlation may be inverse for direct selling (long appointments don't sell – short ones do). They may be right. Try to find out the correlations in your business and it may show you where to focus.

In retail selling, the correlation between time and buying was studied by Paco Underhill described in his book *'Why we buy'*. What he looked at was the average time a shopper spent in the store. He found a strong direct correlation with the amount of time spent in store and the value of purchases.

It seems really obvious – if you are not going to buy something, then you will leave quickly. I wonder if it is the same for shops such as antique centres where you get a lot of 'browsers'.

If there is a correlation in your business, then do you need to give prospects time (direct correlation) or hurry them up (inverse correlation).

When I talked to one group about this, a manager asked if I could help with one of his salespeople. She spent hours with customers. People even said to her, 'You have spent so much time with me, I couldn't possibly buy from anyone else.'

I asked him about her performance compared with colleagues. Both her sales levels and her profitability were outstanding. I couldn't really believe this conversation. He had a salesperson doing an outstanding job and he still wanted to criticise? He was thinking if he could cut down the time spent, she could see more people and increase her sales.

It doesn't work like that I'm afraid. If he cut away the very reason she gets sales, he would affect her sales levels and profitability.

102

87 Practical Tips for Dynamic Selling

Time also works in business-to-business. I know salespeople who, generally, had longer meetings with customers and weren't as successful as others. On average however, the longer meetings are with buyers.

Touching

There is a strong correlation between touching and buying. Feeling products is a big part of buying something.

I always chuckle to myself when I see a sign – *'All breakages must be paid for'* or *'Please don't touch'*. I think about what happens when something is broken.

I imagine when something gets broken there is a big argument. The shopkeeper doesn't get paid. The argument upsets most of the people in the shop and so the shop owner loses out in many ways.

They lose the broken piece that doesn't get paid for. The customer blames them for an unstable display, in the reach of their children etc. They lose custom because people in the shop leave rather than watch the commotion. They lose because the people who did break something never come back.

And they get fewer sales because there is a high correlation between touching and buying.

The daft thing is, if someone breaks something in a shop and the assistant runs up with a bucket to clear it away, they take the responsibility for the breakage away from the customer. You will often see people offering to pay and I have even seen people making a small purchase. I think this works because of reciprocation (see tip no 41)

This applies to all types of selling – get people involved by touching. Never show how anything works – explain and get the prospect to touch. Use models in business-to-business.

Even insurance salespeople can take brochures. Hand over the brochure and get them touching! (see also tip no 35 – *Two Brochures*).

Being touched

There is a strong correlation between physical contact and buying. This tip is likely to cause more problems for people of my generation

103

and those that were born in the country.

People who live in towns don't have the same requirement for body space as people who were born in the country.

In general, younger people are much more tactile.

There seems to be a way for 'non-threatening touch'. We don't seem to take notice when touched between our shoulders to the tip of our fingers. If, like me, you don't like being touched, you may have noticed you are being touched much more these days.

I don't know this for a fact but I am willing to bet that supermarkets include in their training the need to touch people. Even restaurants are into touching these days. I dined with my wife and a friend recently, and the owner had touched all three of us on the shoulder within two minutes of entering the restaurant.

I met a salesman who in a previous job had sold ladies' shoes. He was uncomfortable with touch. His boss told him he could increase his sales if he learned to touch ladies' feet when helping them on with their shoes.

I had to learn to touch people to start feeling comfortable with it. Be very careful with cross-gender touching – I don't want to be cited in a sexual harassment case!

Involvement

Prospects who are involved buy more. Try to get prospects to do things rather than doing it yourself.

An example of this would be filling in application forms.

Normally the salesperson fills in the application form and the prospect only signs it. Just getting a prospect to complete it can dramatically reduced cancellation rates.

Practical Tip No 37

Three Reasons

I worked with a company who taught the sales people to say to customers 'we want your business' (nothing wrong with that!). They were also trained to ask next, 'what do we have to do to get your business?'

It doesn't take a genius to work out that, if you ask this question, the most common answer will be centred around a better price.

Ask for the three most important things they expect from a supplier. Generally the second thing said is the most accurate.

One delegate on a course was a regional manager. He sat in on lots of training courses, taking notes about what his people were committing to implement. He was very taken by this tip and in between two courses tested it out. This is what he said.

'I went to two customers and one prospect. I asked them what were the three most important things they expected from a supplier? The first customer said low price! I expected that – he always hounds me about price – so I waited. Secondly he said deliveries on time and thirdly he wanted availability of stock. The discussion then centred on delivery and stock, and price was never mentioned again. We picked up more business because one of the stock problems was something we had never supplied him with.' He continued, 'The second customer said product quality, secondly frequent deliveries on time and thirdly he wanted visibility of stock on the internet. When I showed him how to see stock on the internet, he was amazed.'

'With the prospect, he never even mentioned price. He said stock availability, daily deliveries and a personality. Someone that would deal with him all the time and get to know him. I took him into the warehouse and introduced him to the counter salesperson and the delivery driver. He placed an order right there and then. I had been chasing him with special offers for ages.'

Asking for three things doesn't remove the request for lower prices but it gives you something else to work with. Your discussion will now move from price – that you can't do anything about – to things that you can achieve.

Practical Tip No 38

Forget the Concept of Loyalty

As far as I am concerned, the concept of loyalty is a dying art.
This is so because:

1. Companies have no loyalty to me as a customer. See Advice no. 83 *Savers*. Banks have no loyalty to me. They would rather encourage a new customer. When I moved my business banking, the new company, HSBC, offered me 6 months' free banking if I moved to them.

    The daft thing about this is I was offered only 6 months because of two things:
    - I was an existing personal customer.
    - I had an established business which has a history and is never overdrawn. If I had been more risky, i.e. a new business with no history, I would have got 12 months' free banking!

2. Companies have no loyalty to me as an employer (or as a consultant for that matter!)

Anyone who has been made redundant will know that if the company doesn't make profit, you must go. I believe the move to contract workers is about disloyalty to employees. It is easier to sack a contract worker.

I am not complaining about this. I am quite happy with it. My company needs to make profit as well. It is the only reason for existing, We are not a charity. If we don't make profit we cease to exist.

The mission, vision and values statement of some companies amuses me. 'We want to serve the community!!' The first value is profit and when a company ceases to do that, with the best will in the world, they need to take steps to address that situation.

Companies have trained people to be price sensitive and so more people are price sensitive. Come to us and we will give you a discount!

87 Practical Tips for Dynamic Selling

Companies have been running training courses about taking responsibility, empowerment, adding value etc. Employees are taking responsibility for their own lives by being self-employed!

Young people of today have less loyalty. I think it will cause two things. Firstly it will cause companies to strive towards having a great product with great service. Secondly it will cause companies to focus once again on Selling Skills. If there is no loyalty, then *all* business has to be sold.

My tip is to focus on repeat business rather than loyalty. Loyalty implies to me that a customer will remain with you through thick and thin. Repeat business means you have to be thick!

If you want repeat business, you must maintain contact, solve problems, learn about customers businesses and be proactive.

In this 'the age of the never satisfied customer', you cannot expect them to keep coming to you. You will have to go to the customers.

A number of companies are trying to do so using marketing. I personally got over 100 junk emails per day before installing a spam filter. My letterbox is overflowing.

There is a huge increase in the number of people calling their house (according to their letterbox) 'No Junk Mail Please'!

To keep in contact will need people – salespeople. They will have to have the skill and relationship that allows them to add value in order to get past the mail filters. Repeat business will have to be sold with as much care and effort as new business.

Practical Tip No 39

Deal with the Behaviour

I explained dealing with behaviour in my first book *'Emotional Selling'*. I will give a very brief review and update here.

I work on behaviours rather than personality although on most courses people seem to confuse the two. The small problems this may cause are easily outweighed by the benefits of dealing differently with the four types (see below).

I categorise behaviour based on two scales.

1. How important is time to people – do they need to get results quickly?
2. How friendly are they. Do they want to get involved with salespeople or are salespeople a necessary evil?

One question I am regularly asked on courses is how do you spot the four different types?

I don't actually analyse people as I meet with them, I don't even think of the strategy for dealing with each behaviour type during a meeting. When I am selling, I deal with people in my normal way, most of us do.

The only time that I think of the behaviour model is when things are not going as well as I would like. When this happens, I try to keep a central thought in my head to get the meeting back on track. I will share with you the signals I get and my central thoughts for each of the four types.

I base the behaviours on the model opposite:

87 Practical Tips for Dynamic Selling

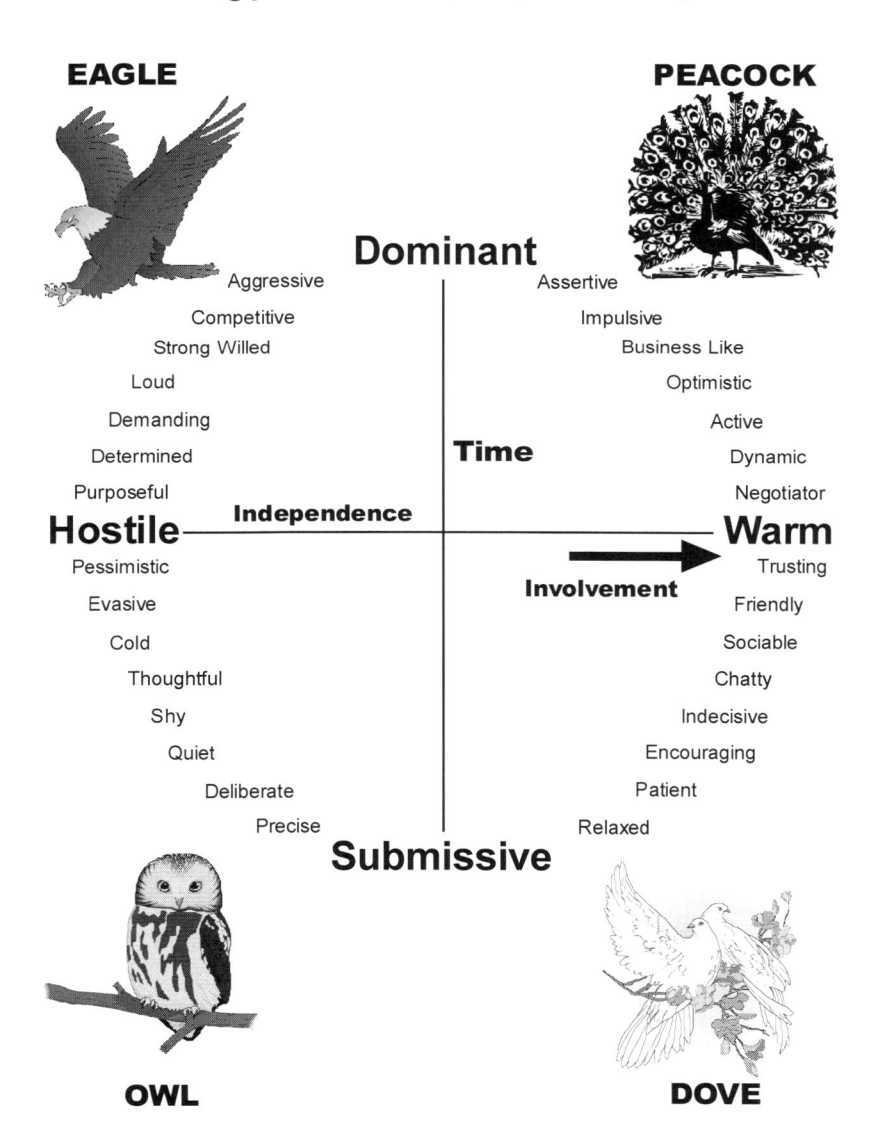

EAGLE

PEACOCK

Dominant

Aggressive	Assertive
Competitive	Impulsive
Strong Willed	Business Like
Loud	Optimistic
Demanding	Active
Determined	**Time**	Dynamic
Purposeful		Negotiator

Hostile ——— Independence ——————→ **Warm**

Involvement

Pessimistic	Trusting
Evasive	Friendly
Cold	Sociable
Thoughtful	Chatty
Shy	Indecisive
Quiet	Encouraging
Deliberate	Patient
Precise	Relaxed

Submissive

OWL

DOVE

109

87 Practical Tips for Dynamic Selling

Dealing with the four types

Eagles

Signal
The signal I get with an Eagle is that they are controlling me. They are asking me questions that cause me to be working on what they want to talk about when they want to talk about it. For example, the Eagle may ask about discounts or lowest prices when I want to be looking at needs and product differentiation.

In fact, Eagles often start buying conversations by discussing prices. I want to start selling conversations with needs and wants.

Dealing with them
You should focus on asking questions about the future and avoid, as far as possible, questions about the present and past.

Remember every salesperson will ask the Eagle factual questions. 'How many of these do you want?' 'How many of that do you want?'

The Eagle gets bored with factual questions about the past. You get some evidence of this because the Eagle will often pre-prepare a list of requirements. It saves them time going through the answers to the factual questions.

Interrupting an Eagle is not a great strategy. You can if you are a product expert, have a higher perceived status than they have or are physically bigger than them!

They are not interested in my opinion, and so I try to avoid the phrases 'I think' or 'I don't think' with them. They don't want to know what I think – they want facts.

Often, they ask for your opinion but they only want your opinion if it is the same as theirs. Giving your opinion is risky. Sometimes they have only asked you to trap you!

A good example of a situation is when my wife asks me whether I prefer the red dress or the blue dress? If I say the red one she would ask 'what is wrong with the blue one?' Although she is asking for my opinion she doesn't want it. I can hear the ladies thinking now, hang on a minute there. When I ask for my husband's opinion, I do want it.

87 Practical Tips for Dynamic Selling

I can give you some evidence you probably don't. You see, most men have the same opinion. We don't care! I tried many different answers with my ex-wife:

'I couldn't care less what you wear – just hurry up!' (Not a good answer I can tell you!)

'Wear the blue one – it goes with your varicose veins' (even worse!)

What I eventually recognised (with the current Mrs Yule!) was that she doesn't really want my opinion.

If she (or an Eagle) asks for my opinion, I use the one-second rule (tip no 29) or I answer them with a Future Opinion question. From my wife's perspective that means asking 'What were you thinking of wearing with them?' 'Who else do you think will be going?' 'What do you think they will be wearing?' Better answers if you take my advice!

I think Eagles are very price sensitive and so I don't play games when pricing, I give them the price and stick to it. I don't think they like people to back down.

They will consider a salesperson to be effective if the salesperson does anything to save them time. Waste their time at your peril.

Central thought

Because they don't particularly like past questions, my central thought is to ask them questions about the future. 'How do you see the market changing?' 'What concerns do you envisage on this contract?' 'What do you think the impact of doing this will be?' etc.

Owls

Signals

The Owl's favourite tactic is to get sales people to answer their own questions. For example, you ask any of the future questions above, you will find the answer is 'I'm not sure' or 'I don't know'. Very soon you will be telling them your thoughts.

Another signal when cold calling would be that they are happy with their existing supplier and don't want to get in to a discussion about it. (see tip no 40 – *Spare Tyre*)

Dealing with them

For Owls, you have to start with Past Fact questions then move to Past Opinion questions.

Some examples of Past Facts questions are, 'Where did you buy your existing product?' How long have you had it?'

Examples of Past Opinion questions are, 'What attracted you to the existing product?' 'What were you looking for when you choose your existing supplier?'

Don't be surprised if the one-second rule (tip no 29) becomes a three-second rule with Owls.

Central thought

Because of their ability to avoid answering questions I use Past Fact questions then move to Past Opinion questions. These are the hardest for them to avoid answering.

Doves

Signals

A Dove manages to combine not objecting with not buying.

I often recognise I am dealing with a Dove but for the most part I don't need to do anything different. They often stray from the point but then so do I. I am sure you will agree with this given that you have read even some of this book!

The only time I need to think differently is when they say they are going to buy, but not now for various reasons, e.g. they need to think about it, they will buy next week. They tell me that everything is wonderful and they will definitely buy later.

Dealing with them

Deal with a dove as you would any friend.

It is okay to interrupt them. An observer would call it interacting with them. If you don't interact with them, you will be seen as interrogating them.

To build rapport with a dove, you can use what psychologists describe as progressive self-disclosure. What they found is that when

87 Practical Tips for Dynamic Selling

we make friends we tend to disclose information about ourselves progressively.

First we disclose on a very factual level. Our name, where we live, our job, our family etc. If we want to develop a closer friendship, we disclose at a more deep and meaningful level. If both parties are happy, then they may go to the next level. Eventually you may get to what women, at least, describe as 'best friend' level.

Females have a tendency to describe their best friend as someone they share their deepest secrets with. For a woman, it is this intimacy that counts. Never mind that they do not see each other for months or even years. For a man, 'best friend' status is usually linked to time spent with the person.

There are business rules to disclosure. You wouldn't expect to go to a doctor and say, 'I have pain in my back,' and expect the doctor to say, 'Yes, my back is killing me as well!' You wouldn't go to a bank manager and say, 'I am overdrawn this month,' and hear the bank manager say, 'Yes, me too, I have had a lot of bills all at once recently!'

A perfect way to disclose with a Dove is using the phrases 'I shouldn't really be saying this to you but ...' or 'Please don't tell my boss I told you this but ...'

You would expect a friend to tell you his or her opinion and if you are to develop a friendship with a dove, then using your opinion is one way of doing so. You can combine it with the above. 'I shouldn't really be saying this, but the less expensive one is just as good for you, because ...'

Central thought

Close them or lose them. When I do a behaviour model exercise on courses, most delegates think the dove is the most loyal of the four behaviour types.

This may be true, personality wise, but you need to close them or lose them. If you don't, someone else will.

To close them I need to find hidden objections and for this I use reciprocity (see tip no 41 – *Reciprocity*) and then perhaps I need to '*Create and Objection*' (see tip no83)

Peacocks

Signals
The signal I look for with a peacock is a negotiation. It is a different style of negotiation from those with an Eagle. With the Peacock, I think everything is going well – I am getting a sale. Suddenly at the very end, I am surprised by a request for discount. It is usually done in a very friendly way.

Dealing with them
I don't think you need to do anything special with a peacock except be careful when you think they are wrong (see tip no 19 – *People don't like to be proved wrong*)

Central thought
My central thought with a peacock is to keep some margin up my sleeve. Never leave yourself with nowhere to go. A negotiation will come.

Practical Tip No 40

Spare Tyre

I use this technique when I call a prospect and they say they are happy with their existing supplier.

I use a little story! Selling using stories should be a tip all on its own.

'I am sure you are happy with your existing supplier. It wouldn't make sense to buy from someone you weren't happy with. That is exactly the loyalty we look for from our customers. I would recommend if you have a good relationship and get good service to stay with your existing supplier. I wouldn't mind betting that on your car, although you have four good tyres, you still keep a spare tyre in the boot. I would like to be your spare tyre. I promise I won't attack the relationship you have with your existing suppliers but if they let you down I would like to be able to help you. Would it be okay to go on that basis?'

I have never had anyone turn me down after saying this.

Now let's look at the figures. A study showed that after 8 contacts, 83% of prospects have placed an order with you. The same study showed that 80% of salespeople give up within the first 3 contacts. Over 20% give up after the first contact.

Because the success rate is low in the first three contacts, most salespeople do the hard work and then give up.

Look at the success curve overleaf. In the first three contacts, only 17 out of 100 prospects bought. That means you have made 300 contacts (100 prospects 3 times each) and only had 17 orders. From the 4th to the 6th contact is where the major success is achieved. This means for maximum efficiency you don't need to sell in the first three contacts. You should be as good as your word and not attack the existing suppliers.

Incidentally, most salespeople try to teach prospects that are not price sensitive to be price sensitive. When they contact prospects,

Propects Placing Orders

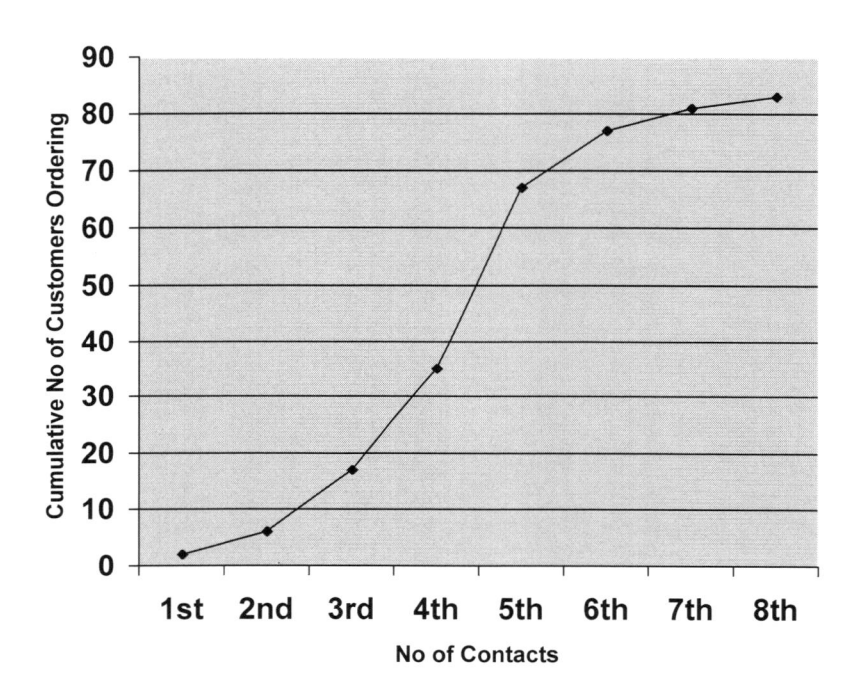

Chart: Cumulative No of Customers Ordering vs No of Contacts (1st through 8th), showing values rising from ~2 at 1st contact to ~83 at 8th contact.

they try to reduce the costs and show how they could save money. A better approach is to demonstrate the service you give existing customers.

The problem is that new customers haven't experienced your service. Everybody claims to have great service when they are selling! (see tip no 67 – *Don't do what others do*). Here is a chance to demonstrate the type of service you give to clients.

Here are some good contact reasons.

Good contact reasons

To give them insider information

For example, to tell them a price is going up/down and they

should buy now/not buy now from their existing supplier. Most salespeople use this the wrong way. By this I mean that when the price is going up, they say, 'buy from us today.' This is an attack on the existing supplier.

I recommend contacting and saying, 'I am calling all of my customers to let them know there will be an increase in the price of plastic and that will filter through next month. Can I suggest you go to your existing supplier and buy now if you can handle extra stock.'

You don't need to sell on this call. You are demonstrating the service you give to 'existing customers'. Indeed, sometimes you will be asked for a price and it is better at this time not to commit to a price. Use *Ballpark Figures* (tip no 46).

In the case of a price reduction. 'I am calling all my existing customers to let them know the price of semiconductors is falling. If you can hold off buying this month, you should be able to save on costs.'

Again there is no need to ask for them to buy from you for the same reasons. If you use my strategy you won't need to sell.

Prospects will be impressed at the service you give your customers. They will feel the need to reciprocate (see tip no 41). They will want to give you a small order to thank you (see tip no 30 – *Go for small orders*).

To give them a lead for their business

Many salespeople feel uncomfortable about this because they feel they should be supporting existing customers and give them extra leads. Hard to disagree with that one! If you can use this, I can assure you it is the fastest way to converting a prospect.

Supplier information/presentation evenings

Many companies organise supplier presentations to give additional help to end users. Even bookshops use writers (I am available on request!) to sell books.

New products and developments

A word of caution about the effect of phantom products, i.e. products that are not yet available. Never tell an existing customer of a product that isn't available yet.

I have had many arguments with sales managers and marketing managers about this. As soon as a new product is announced, the sales of the existing product plummet. It makes it harder to forecast when to introduce the new product. From personal experience, it also makes it harder to sell the old product. How can you face someone saying this is the best when you know the best is yet to come!

Bad contact reasons

- Because you had nothing else to do or were just passing. I even saw a salesperson tell a prospect they were filling time before a really important appointment nearby. Don't laugh – this is serious!
- Just to keep in touch (you are just wasting everyone's time).
- Because their name came to the top of your contact list!
- To find out if they need anything. If they need something they will contact you.
- To introduce yourself or others.
- Here is some good advice; never tell anyone of your problems. Half the world don't care about your problems. The other half are glad you have the problem! They don't care about you or anybody else in your organisation. You are trying to develop a relationship with them. They aren't with you. You will be much more successful if you focus on their needs rather than yours.
- Any blatant attack on their existing suppliers (e.g. special deals etc.)

Practical Tip No 41

Reciprocity

Human beings have a need to reciprocate.

In an experiment, a person working in an office was asked to treat colleagues in two ways.

- With one group of colleagues they were asked to be very helpful, getting coffee, helping with filing and doing errands etc. generally to be thoughtful and helpful.
- With another group they were asked to be polite and friendly. But, if they were asked for help from them, to make an excuse to avoid helping.

At the end of the week, the person was asked to sell raffle tickets and you can guess which side bought more raffle tickets.

Our need to reciprocate increases with the strength of what the person does for us, i.e. how difficult it was for them to do the task. If someone smiles at us we need to reciprocate and smile back but if we really put ourselves out, people feel they 'owe us something'.

The need to reciprocate is why doing things 'without obligation' still leaves most people feeling obligated.

Sometimes the need to reciprocate makes life difficult for us. For example, when a client has dealt with another supplier over some years, they feel a loyalty to the existing supplier in return for the years of perceived good service.

Customers will tend to go back to their existing supplier with your quote and use it as a negotiation tool rather than give you the business.

Some ways of minimising the chances of this are:

1. Get the prospect to examine the habit with questions about service. (see tip no 42 – *Competition*)
2. Use consistency questions to pre-close. E.g. 'What action would

87 Practical Tips for Dynamic Selling

you take if we provided you with a more attractive option?' 'How would you feel about leaving your existing supplier?'
3. Get commitment before providing full details. Use ballpark figures and general details until getting commitment. (see tip no 51 – *Letters of Intent*)
4. Use reciprocation by letting them see how much time effort and costs are involved in getting final quotations.

In relationship terms, reciprocity can be used to get information from clients. If clients feel you have gone out of your way to help them, use the need to reciprocate to get introductions to other parts of their business and more opportunities to expand the range of services provided to a client.

I use reciprocity to find out whether there is a hidden objection.

When dealing with doves (see tip no 39 – *Deal with the Behaviour*), I find they are able to combine not objecting with not buying. To work with an example of this, let me use 'I need to think about it' (see also tip no 11 – *Think*)

I have used the one-second rule and gained little. I would now use reciprocation.

Let me give a practical example to explain. Imagine you are selling a car and the customer wants to think about it. This is very sensible, it is probably the second biggest purchase of his life. The biggest purchase is generally buying a house. I read somewhere that the average person buying a house makes the decision to go ahead within 20 minutes. Think about it, I say.

The difficulty from a sales perspective is this – does the prospect want to think about it or has he almost decided not to buy and is using this as a way out? Is there a hidden objection?

What if the salesperson agreed it was a big decision and thanked the prospect for thinking about it. It is, after all, what the salesperson wants. What if he then offered something that would be extremely helpful and invoke the need to reciprocate? For example, what if he offered to let the prospect take the car home for the evening or weekend?

If you do this, then you need to watch the reaction carefully.

87 Practical Tips for Dynamic Selling

People with a hidden objection will never consider taking the car home for an instant.

If they say they would like to take the car home you can almost guarantee they will come back the next day!

Car salespeople I have discussed this strategy with come up with all the reasons they can't do this. For example what if the car isn't taxed? I am not suggesting you actually give them the car. I am only saying you offer it to test their reaction.

Other things you could do are to get the product in stock for them to see it, place it on pre-order with the manufacturer. Put it aside for them because it is your last one and there is a high demand etc. The more trouble you go to, the greater the need for reciprocity.

With doves you may also consider using this with some personal disclosure 'I shouldn't really do this for you but …' (see tip no 39 – *Deal with the behaviour – Doves*)

Rejection then retreat

A good example of the use of reciprocity is the rejection then retreat technique.

This is used in a negotiation. First of all you propose something that you know is unacceptable and wait until it gets rejected. Then you offer to make a concession. In negotiations, concessions are most likely to be met with concessions from the other party.

This is because you have made a concession, they feel the need to reciprocate. It also uses comparison theory making the second proposal seem less unacceptable than the first (rejected) proposal.

It is thought that the Watergate affair in America was only accepted because of rejection then retreat. The sponsor had suggested many other schemes which were even more outrageous. (For a full explanation see tip no28 – *Cialdini*!!)

Practical Tip No 42

Competition

Always compliment the competition. This is using child psychology.

Most salespeople know that they shouldn't criticise the competition. Criticising them would be like asking a customer, 'What idiot would buy from them?'

What most salespeople don't seem to be aware of is *implied* criticism of the competition.

For example, the question, 'How do you find their service?' can be an implied criticism. It implies that they are poor with their service. Just asking the question also implies that you believe that your service is better than theirs. If you didn't think your service was better, you wouldn't ask the question.

Almost every time I have heard this question, the prospect has defended the service of the competitor.

A better strategy is to compliment the competition. Strangely, I have found when I go over the top, it works best.

For example the prospect says, 'I use xyz company'. My response is 'I don't know a lot about them but other customers of mine have told me they do an excellent job, their products never break down and they are always on time with deliveries.'

Two things can happen. If the competitor is brilliant, your chances of getting the business were slim anyway and I don't think you have harmed them.

If the service they are getting isn't great – and that is my experience – the prospect starts to criticise them. 'They aren't that brilliant! They do let me down!' Just what you were hoping for – an opportunity. Don't jump on it or the prospect will spot the tactic you used. Play it slowly. I recommend using the spare tyre analogy at this time (see tip no 40).

What is implied in this situation is:

87 Practical Tips for Dynamic Selling

1. The prospect isn't as important to your competitor as their other customers (the ones that are receiving the great service!).
2. I am not concerned about a competitor's superb service – it only matches ours.
3. Finally, because I used 'customers', it is implied that people who dealt with them now deal with me. That may be because they changed or because they buy from both of us.

Practical Tip No 43

Windows of Opportunity

Reproduced with the kind permission of Peter Thompson (Achievers Edge)

Whoever said 'telling isn't selling' was wrong. If you look at why your customers don't buy everything from you, it is because they don't know everything you sell.

Get together with some colleagues and try writing down individually what products or services your company sells. Then compare notes. Most people I work with forget some products. If you find it difficult, how can you expect your customers to remember?

The Windows of Opportunity helps you to plan a strategy of consistently informing customers about your products.

Draw up a chart similar to the one opposite and write your customers' names down the left-hand side and your products along the bottom. Block out the products they currently buy.

Systematically tell people about the products they don't buy at the moment. Give them a presentation on one product they don't buy, at every meeting. It makes meetings more interesting as well.

At each meeting you can set up the next presentation.

Beware if the customer asks for information now. For example, you say, 'I want to let you know about our relays next time I call.' The customer responds with, 'Oh, that would be good – can you tell me about them now?' My tip is not to. Just find out what they need.

I have already fallen foul of this. Somehow the waiting increases the desire. If you go straight to your car and get out your relays, you will almost never sell them.

I have even had the customer desperate for me to show them here and now and wanting to buy. When I showed them, I never got an order. I don't know why this is but the waiting does increase the desire.

Window of Opportunity

Client		Asset Management	Tax Reporting	E-banking	Global Custody	Translation
	ABC Company	SOLD		SOLD		
	XYZ Company				SOLD	SOLD
	ACME Company		SOLD			
	Grabbit & Run		SOLD			
	Toy Factory			SOLD		SOLD

For each client enter:
Told date / Sold date

Product or Service

Practical Tip No 44

It Is Better Not To Do Something Than Do It Badly

That goes for lots of things.

Corporate Entertaining
I worked with an American company. When I went to France for a meeting with the top managers of a prospect, I took them for lunch. My American boss insisted I should observe the company policy on alcohol. I insisted it is better *not* to take a French person out for lunch than to take them and try to prevent them from drinking wine.

Small Talk
If you find small talk very difficult, it is better just to get down to business. Small talk is supposed to relax people. There is no point in doing so if you feel nervous and make the other person embarrassed.

Humour
I use a lot of humour in selling. If you are not a naturally 'funny' person, using humour is a disaster. I can hear people reading this book and saying to themselves, 'If what you have written is trying to pass for humour, what makes you think you are funny?'

I won't answer because you are probably right!

Practical Tip No 45

Fake Your Attitude

I have some weird views on body language. I don't think it is possible to fake your body language.

Body language is too complex to fake. While you are faking one thing, the rest of your body is screaming the truth.

In a study about telling lies, researchers found that even children as young as 3 years old made eye contact when lying. The trouble is we now read excessive eye contact as a signal of not telling the truth!

An article in the *Psychologist* magazine considered 'pacing'. The term is used to describe developing rapport through copying the body language of another person. They concluded that pacing is more likely to make rapport harder to develop. Overt pacing is likely to prevent rapport.

What *can* be faked is attitude. It is much easier as well. When you fake your attitude, your body language follows.

I can make myself believe people are interesting, sincere, honest and so on. Because of confirmation bias (see tip no 3), they usually are as well.

Practical Tip No 46

Use Ballpark Figures

If you have customers asking for a discount, then this is the best way I know of stopping it.

You may need some imagination to apply it to your business. I will explain the scenario that the salesperson is working in a bathroom showroom and all the products have a label with the retail price on.

I approach the prospect and give an overview. In the overview (see tip no17 – *Overviews*), I have set up using ballpark figures. I have said I will work out a rough cost and then if that is okay, I will price it up accurately.

Now I have the prospect wandering around the showroom. They are asking questions about products, commenting on what they like and don't like. At some point, I will stop them and say, 'Let me get some rough figures on costs for you.'

'Based on what you have been saying, if you took that bath with that WC and this washbasin, by the time you add taps, fittings, waste etc, you are probably looking at £1,700. How does that sound?'

There are two possible answers – it's either okay or it isn't. Listen very carefully and if you get a 'maybe' here, then you are still at the finding needs stage.

If the answer is that £1,700 sounds okay, then you move to the decision stage. 'Now I need you to make some decisions and I can price everything up for you.' When you price everything up, provided you are under £1,700, they will find it much harder to ask for a discount. They have already agreed that £1,700 is fine. Why would they ask for a discount now?

NB – I am not trying to suggest this is a failsafe way of preventing people asking for a discount. Magic wands are out of stock just now! It just makes it harder for them to ask.

The secret is of course to get the final price to be below £1,700. If the prospect went on to choose the most expensive taps, you would

87 Practical Tips for Dynamic Selling

immediately say 'If you go for these taps you would now be looking at £2,000.'

If you make a mistake and the final price comes in at over £1,700 you have encouraged the customer to ask for a discount. They will ask even if they are the type of people who don't like doing so.

Let's look at the other option. If they say £1,700 is too high when you give the ballpark, the discussion will now naturally turn to less expensive products rather than discounts. Also, because you have told them in the overview that they didn't need to make any firm decisions before you give them the ballpark figure, there is no need for them to back down.

Using ballpark figures is very easy if the products are not priced.

Always use ballpark figures with customers that simply use you for quotations. Some clients give you the opportunity to tender but your chances of getting the business are very low. You may even have quoted lots of times before and not won any of them.

Usually they have a preferred supplier and they use your proposal as a negotiation tool with them.

Use ballpark figures to increase your chance.

Give them a rough idea of the cost and terms and ask them if they want you to price up accurately. If they do, then this is when you need to go for commitment prior to pricing accurately.

I use reciprocity (tip no 41) as well. Explain to them the expense of pricing up accurately. If you believe there is a good chance of getting the business if you provide the best proposal, you would be prepared to invest heavily in terms of time and effort to make sure you have the best proposal. In order to do that, you need some commitment that they are prepared to give you the business.

A letter of intent is a brilliant tool here (see tip no51).

Practical Tip No 47

Implied v Explicit

Experiments have shown that implied statements are more powerful than explicit statements.

One of the things the experimenters were trying to show was the effect of a judge telling a jury to disregard some evidence. The effect was that the jury would place more emphasis on that evidence than if the judge hadn't requested that the jury disregard it!

The judge telling them to disregard it had the effect of implying it was crucial evidence. It was also doubly powerful because they thought they were privy to some information they weren't supposed to have.

The power of an implied statement is that, when someone hears an explicit claim, the thought process is about it being incorrect. For example, if I said I am the best Sales Trainer in the world, you would be thinking about the things in the book that you disagree with. You may also think about other trainers, maybe even yourself, who are better.

The explicit claim has a tendency to cause people to think negatively.

I sort implied and explicit into three groups.

There are explicit facts

'We have 26 branches all over the UK and 300 branches throughout the world.' This is an explicit fact. It implies things about your organisation – big, successful, lots of other people buy from you etc.

Next, explicit claims

'Best pizza in town.' 'Biggest stock in the UK.' I have noticed that some companies haven't really got the hang of 'best'.

87 Practical Tips for Dynamic Selling

Then you have implied statements
Implied statements are designed to get the listener/reader to work it out for themselves. If they do work it out themselves, they will defend their own conclusion. Remember – people don't like to be proved wrong (tip no 19).

Product Range
Top organisations choose a supplier with an extensive product range (this implies, because you are saying it, that your product range is extensive). This implied statement can be adjusted to suit your product range, e.g. the most innovative product range or a value oriented product range etc.

Conventional Approach
Let's say you want to propose a solution that is new to the market place. Your competitor doesn't have your product. Set this up by saying, 'The conventional approach to providing a solution is to … (explain the product your competitor will recommend!)'. *Conventional* implies that there is a newer, better way of going about it.

Cheap
Their *cheapest* solution (cheap implies all sorts of things as well as cost); our *least expensive* solution; our *highest value* solution. Never use the word 'cheap' to describe your products. Only use 'cheap' when acknowledging competitors' products.

If your prices are higher and you are successful, it implies the people who are buying from you know something others don't. Never be frightened by someone telling you a competitor is cheaper.

If a customer tells me that someone is cheaper, I usually acknowledge that I know there are cheaper products available in the market place.

Of course you need a different strategy if you believe you are selling exactly the same product as your competitors (see tip no 78 – *Differentiators*). In this case, you may also use implied statements to move them from the similar product to an exclusive range. If you use an explicit statement, e.g. there are quality problems with that range, prospects are suspicious. Rightly, as you are saying that you sell poor quality products.

An example of using an explicit statement could be, 'We used to sell a lot more of them but now we sell more of these.' Give the customer the opportunity to ask you why rather than offering an explanation – being asked is much more powerful. When asked, use an implied statement, e.g. 'We chose to support this manufacturer and have never had a single product quality issue with them.'

Experience
'Experience shows that is a very complicated situation and I would like to go back to the office and discuss it with an expert.' It is very easy to recommend the wrong solution for this. If your competitors spout answers from the top of their heads, the clients will feel they haven't understood the issue correctly.

Different
For some reason, we all like to believe we are different. On courses, people often come to me in a break to discuss their situation. I have had delegates tell me they are different from all of the other delegates. Their products are 'the best in the market' or 'not good quality' or 'high priced' or 'low price' or their customers are particularly 'price sensitive' or they work in a 'poor area' or a 'rich area' and so their customers are not price sensitive. We all like to be thought of as different and will tend to believe the salesperson who tells us that we are different and complex.

Problem
Any statement that suggests there is a problem with other products implies that your product does not have that problem. Don't mention a competitor – as that would make it an explicit statement.

Words which imply things:

| Recent study | Cheap | Conventional |
| Traditional | Modern | Popular |

Practical Tip No 48

Sell The Brand

When I observe salespeople, the only thing that I have heard them say about the brand is, 'It's a good brand'.

If you consider the last tip (*Implied v Explicit*) the brand should be implying lots of things and, as a salesperson, your job is to sell the brand.

In tip no 57 – *Control, Influence, Concern,* I mention an exercise that I do when I ask salespeople how they could improve sales. Almost always top of their list is more advertising.

Some companies spend huge amounts of money using the poorest forms of advertising and ignore the most powerful form. The most powerful form of advertising is 'word of mouth'. Because, generally, Sales and Marketing departments don't work together closely enough, most salespeople have very little idea about selling their brand.

My prediction is that in the future, because the amount of information available to us is increasing, the value of formal advertising will diminish. Companies will have to turn to salespeople to advertise the brand.

For me, the strongest brands were created when there were only three television channels and a handful of papers and magazines. Today there are literally thousands of each with Satellite television and the internet.

Brands are built around what marketers describe as the 'Brand Values'. What does the brand represent? There are two methods of obtaining brand values.

- Marketing people sit in a room and decide the brand values, and then try to convince the public about them through advertising. (The very, very expensive way).

133

87 Practical Tips for Dynamic Selling

- You go and ask the public what words they think of when they hear your name. (If the words are ones you like, this is less expensive).

The difficulty with the second method is that sometimes the brand values you discover are not the ones you want. For example if, ten years ago, Skoda asked the public what words they think about when they hear 'Skoda', what responses do you think they would have got? They needed to resort to the expensive method and create different brand values.

To give an example of how to sell a brand, you need to know the brand values. Let's take as an example a Saab car. When Saab asked the public what words came to mind when they hear the word SAAB, one of the things that came out consistently was Aircraft Heritage.

When selling a Saab, it would be useful to point out things that came from their aircraft heritage. For example, the aircraft industry investigates major accidents. As a result of Saab's aircraft heritage, they investigate major accidents. The innovations that have sprung from accident investigations (according to Saab) have been superb.

Here are some of the innovations resulting from Saab investigating major accidents:

- The 'moose test' which is now used as an industry standard. This is where a vehicle weaves in and out to avoid hitting something. You may remember a Ford advert that showed a car driving towards a moose. Saab invented this test, as a result of an investigation, after their own MD was killed in an accident when his car struck a moose.
- Daytime running lamps (now perhaps more associated with Volvo).
- Side Impact Protection System (again more associated with Volvo)
- Crumple zones so the car gets more damage but the driver gets less.
- Hinging the engine so it goes underneath you in a head-on collision rather than through you.
- Active airbags where the airbag only half inflates in certain circumstances. Saab discovered many injuries were being caused by the airbags.
- Anti-whiplash seats to prevent whiplash injuries.

87 *Practical Tips for Dynamic Selling*

- The ignition key in a different place from other manufacturers in order to avoid injuring your knees in an accident.

You may be thinking this is a Saab advert but my ex-next door neighbour is a Saab fanatic. Thanks to Sid Gibson.

The point of this tip is that you need to find out what your own products' brand values are and then use them in your selling. Use the values to support your selling and strengthen the brand. The brand values are a powerful way of implying without explicitly stating.

Practical Tip No 49

Half Empty or Half Full

I wonder what type of person would buy a product because it could be fixed it if it broke down. I read a mystery shop report once, (you can see what I think of mystery shopping in tip no 3 –v *Confirmation Bias*), where the shopper said, 'The salesperson explained all about the guarantee but, when I thought about it, I didn't much like the idea of my appliance breaking down.'

After that, I started looking carefully about what type of people like guarantees. It led me to a whole new strategy.

I found that people who see a glass with water in as half-full or half empty are interested in different things.

People who see the glass as *half full* are excited by the words:

New
Exclusive
Exciting
Trial offer
End of Line
Increase
Improve
Gain

People who see the glass as *half empty* are motivated more easily using:

Guaranteed
Brand names
Most popular
Savings
Reductions

I also found that sometimes I see the glass as half full and sometimes half empty. It depends on the product I am buying. For example, when I buy a new computer, I see the glass as half empty. I am worried about it breaking down and the technical support and warranties seem important. When buying a vacuum cleaner, I certainly see the glass as half full and don't care about guarantees.

I guess this comes from previous experience with these products. I have never had a vacuum cleaner that broke down. I have always needed technical support on every computer I have bought (and some software programmes too).

How do you tell them apart? Very easily – people that see the glass as half full will tend to point out what they like when you are presenting products. People who see the glass as half empty will tend to point out what they don't like.

When presenting to people who see the glass as half full, you should mention the guarantee but not make a big thing of it. You may think that saying you have a five-year guarantee implies better quality. You are right and you are also implying the product does break down.

When presenting to people who see the glass as half empty you should mention the stability and popularity of the product.

If you have a new exciting product, you may wish to stress the size and quality of the manufacturer.

'End of line' is an interesting one. The end of line can be presented as tried and tested technology. It can also be presented as out of date with spares being a difficulty. You can put the slant based on the product and your objectives.

Practical Tip No 50

Commitment and Consistency

Consistency is the DOOR, Commitment is the KEY

People have a need for consistency, they do not like to contradict themselves. Nor do we like people to see us in a way that is inconsistent with our values and beliefs.

Inconsistency is seen to be an undesirable personality trait – inconsistent people are seen as confused, two-faced or even mentally ill. Consistency is a powerful motivator.

Let me illustrate ways in which using people's need for consistency can increase sales.

The desire to satisfy a need increases when the need has been stated aloud. Some questions that ask the customer to confirm their needs out loud and help you to use their need for consistency are:

- ? 'Do you look for Lowest Price or Best Value?'
- ? 'Is it better waiting for the best quality or do you need something in a hurry?'
- ? 'Do you want the conventional approach or are you looking for exceptional results?'
- ? 'Do you prefer traditional or modern styles?'
- ? 'Have you found that buying cheap costs you dearly?'
- ? 'Are you worried about offending potential customers?'
- ? 'Are you looking for an "off the shelf" product or something tailored to your clients?'

You may notice these are all closed questions! (See tip no 20 – *Open and Closed Questions*). They are all questions where the answers are probably fairly predictable. Because of this they are often left unasked.

87 Practical Tips for Dynamic Selling

To use commitment, you have to make the implicit explicit

If consistency is the door, then commitment is definitely the key. Cialdini (tip no 28) showed that getting commitment can have up to a 700% increase in effectiveness in getting things done.

Which of these cancel more? Sales with no deposit, sales with a low deposit or fully paid ones?

Commitment works on different levels. In direct selling, getting a deal without a deposit isn't really getting a deal. Getting a small deposit is better, medium deposit better still and so on.

Most salespeople ask for commitment at the end but this is too late. A salesperson should be asking for commitment throughout the sale.

How many people ask you, 'Can you help me please?' and then don't wait for a response?

Waiting for a response, especially with secretaries, telephonists, and gatekeepers, will dramatically increase the success of a request for help.

Before giving a price, go through what you are pricing and get commitment that the product is what they really want. This is using consistency and commitment. There is no point in discussing price on a product that someone doesn't want to buy. If they don't want to buy it, then the price is irrelevant.

Practical Tip No 51

Use Letters of Intent

Too little use is made of letters of intent.

Many companies put their business out to tender every three years or so. For the most part, they are checking the current market conditions. They do it to keep the existing suppliers 'on their toes'.

Because of the costs of preparing competitive quotations, you should only do so if there is a fair chance that you will get the business.

Most salespeople take the attitude that if you are not in the lottery you can't win. This isn't selling, it is firing a blunderbuss and hoping for one hit. Selling is a much more targeted use of resources.

In most cases, taking a stronger stand before putting forward tenders, proposals and so on will pay dividends.

Taking a stronger stand does several things for you:

1. It gets rid of the people who aren't giving you a serious chance of getting the business. This saves time and money to spend on the serious opportunities.

    I did some sales coaching work with a training company. They asked me how to deal with tenders. I said you must get to meet with the prospect and discuss needs with them. They had tried that but the prospects (public companies) had refused. If you can't get a meeting you should refuse to tender.

    It is irresponsible to put forward a proposal without understanding needs fully. I said they should refuse to tender in these situations. Their response was, 'You need to be in to win'. I asked them how many they had won using their strategy – none! In ten years – not one!

    They needed to do something to improve their chances or put their resources elsewhere.

2. It uses consistency and commitment to give you a better chance

of getting the business. (see tip no 50 – *Commitment and Consistency*)

3. It implies you are successful when you bid. (see tip no 47 – *Implied v Explicit*)

4. It gives you an opportunity to explain the costs of tendering (which are covered by existing customers) and invoke reciprocity (see tip no 41).

You would be surprised at how much commitment you can get on most serious opportunities.

I use **letters of intent** for this purpose. A letter of intent states that you will get the business provided you can give them an acceptable solution and improve on what they have just now.

I believe that if the prospect will not sign a letter of intent, it is because I have no chance of getting the business anyway. With genuine opportunities, my experience is that business people understand the need and are willing to become involved in order to secure a better supplier. This also make use of involvement (see tip no 36 – *Correlations*)

Legally, a letter of intent probably has less value than an oral contract (not worth the paper it is written on!). It uses the concept of commitment to increase your chances.

Practical Tip No 52

Do What You Say You Will Do

I have no idea why this seems so hard for people. What is so difficult about saying to people, 'I will call you back by 3 o'clock' and doing so?

Of course, I think the problem is mainly because we make rash promises. Probably for the best of reasons – trying to show how good our service is. All that happens is that the customer sees how *bad* our service is.

My tip is to stop promising when things will happen and start asking people when they need it for.

Explain what has to happen before you call back, e.g. 'I need to speak with the designer and as soon as I can get a hold of him, I will call you back. When do you need the information by?'

Get proposals in by the dates that you promise. If that isn't going to happen, let them know well in advance.

Here is a great tip for success:

Every morning when you get up write down what you want to achieve that day.

Do it!

Practical Tip No 53

Give Bad News in Advance

If you have to give someone bad news, give them it in advance. Saying 'next month there will be a price increase' will avoid lots of heartache. It is better than saying the price went up last month!

Really bad news needs to be told further in advance.

Governments use this strategy.

The government announced an end to duty-free within the EEC. Bad news – so they set it up and said that five years on, there wouldn't be any duty free. No one cared until the day and by then most had accepted the idea.

The same happened with female retiring age moving from 60 to 65. That was *really bad news* and so had to be done 20 years in advance. I am willing to bet that if the government had known there would be so little flak, that they would have increased the retirement age for males and females to 70 years.

Any bad news – price increases, late delivery or whatever – should be given well in advance.

If you are not going to be able to make a delivery, it may be uncomfortable for you, but tell your customer in advance. Do it before the customer has to contact you.

Practical Tip No 54

Don't Upset Browsers

In the first instance, I will use a retail setting to explain, but this tip applies equally to both retail and business-to-business.

When I am running courses (I may have had a Freudian slip here – when I first typed this, I typed 'when I am ruining courses!!').

When I am running courses, I often ask about *browsers*.

I ask how many showrooms does the average shopper enter if he or she wants to buy a bathroom suite. I use bathroom suites because it is the only product I have any data about!

Typically, people will answer 4 to 5 if they live in a city and less if they live in the country.

The actual average figure is 11 showrooms! People are surprised by this. People in the UK normally start off at B&Q and then go looking elsewhere for comparisons.

Salespeople seem to believe that this happens over a fairly short time scale. They also seem to think the reason that people come into the showroom is to see if there is anything they want to buy. They see it as their job to sell to people who want to buy. *This is not how people shop.*

In fact, it usually happens over a period which can be, for some products, as much as two years or more.

I don't know about your short-term memory but I would find it impossible to keep memories of all 11 showrooms in my head. What we do therefore is to try to knock down the list a little. Rather than deciding whether we want to buy, we are knocking potential suppliers off the list.

That way we bring the number of potential suppliers down to a manageable number.

The job of the salesperson is to sell to people who don't want to buy. If someone wants to buy then you facilitate buying rather than sell.

I use three different definitions:

Buying
Customers know what they want and are prepared to pay the price and accept the terms.

No one 'sells' you an airline ticket or a ticket to the theatre. The employee facilitates buying.

Negotiation
The customers know what they want and are not prepared to pay the price or accept the terms.

If the discussion is only about adjusting the price or terms, no one is selling here. Only negotiation is taking place.

Selling
When the customers don't know what they want or cannot see the value of the product, they are therefore undecided about the right product for them and how much they need it.

Only in this scenario does selling take place. This is the job of the salesperson – to help prospects to discover what exactly they need and to highlight the value of the solution to them.

It means that the salesperson's job is to sell to people that don't want to buy from them rather than those that do.

If prospects are trying to reduce their list of potential suppliers to a manageable short list, you can't afford to do anything to upset them. If prospects enter with the sole purpose of getting a brochure or price list and they walk out without a brochure or price list, they generally don't come back.

You may find it strange that anyone could walk into a showroom looking for a brochure and walk out without one. This happens because, I think unbelievably, some businesses hide the brochures and/or price lists so that the customers have to talk to a salesperson. This actually puts the onus and pressure of the approach on to the customer. Today's potential customers simply leave and look it up on the internet. Don't blame them if they buy on the internet!

In businesses, usually the buyer will start off with a potential list

87 Practical Tips for Dynamic Selling

of 7 or 8 suppliers. They may invite all of them to come and have an initial meeting. A short list is drawn up and then two or three companies are invited back to do a final presentation. Then the chosen supplier is usually invited back again to discuss final terms.

The point of this tip depends on whether your job is to facilitate buying (in which case you maybe don't have time to speak with browsers) or selling.

If your job is to facilitate buying, make certain everything a browser may need is prominently displayed. Just beside the door isn't a good place because people don't stop immediately on entering a showroom.

For selling, you need to talk to as many people as possible. Paco Underhill (*Why We Buy*) found people are twice as likely to buy if the salesperson initiates the contact.

Another great rule for selling:

**Speak to as many people as you can.
Ask all of them to buy**

Practical Tip No 55

Never Say No

Always focus on the conditions in which you would say yes.

I was doing some sales training with a famous fabric manufacturer. They had two ranges. Range A was the superior product. They sold through exclusive outlets. For reasons of scarcity, they didn't want too many authorised retailers. Range B was a better than average product and still quite exclusive but they would give an agency for this range to more companies, e.g. designers etc.

Before doing the training I did some field work. I spent a day with their salesman, Nigel. Nigel and I went to see some customers in the North Midlands. We had a very pleasant day together.

In the afternoon, we went to see a customer who had an agency for Range B and Nigel told me she would pester him about getting an agency for Range A. She asked about it every time. Nigel was trying to manage his accounts and he already had a Range A agency in this little town and so, because of exclusivity, wouldn't have two agencies. The other agency had been held for 20 years or more and his firm didn't like to upset them.

I must admit my mouth was watering at the prospect. As a salesperson, I can think of no better situation than having two potential customers both wanting the same thing.

We called at the customer and met the owner. Sure enough, she asked about the agency for Range A and Nigel said that unfortunately he couldn't give her an agency because of exclusivity. He already had an agent in that area.

After a little while, I explained that I didn't work for the company and couldn't promise anything but asked the customer if I could ask some 'daft' questions.

Me: 'If you did get a Range A agency how much business do you think you could do?'
Agent: 'We could guarantee a minimum of £10,000 in the first year'.

87 Practical Tips for Dynamic Selling

That is an okay sum for a top range fabric company, certainly not to be sniffed at.

Me: 'How could you guarantee it?'
Agent: 'Well at the moment we spend that much with Zoffany and I don't like their products as much as Range A. We would immediately transfer all the Zoffany business to you.'

When Nigel and I got back to the car, I asked him to look up his records to see how much business the other agent in this small town had given them the previous year. The figure was a staggering £78!

Nigel was turning down over £10,000's worth of business in order to keep a £78 customer from being offended. Personally, even if I didn't have another potential agency, I would have offended them much sooner!!

The point of this is that when someone asks for something, instead of turning them down, try to explore the conditions under which you would say yes.

Another of my customers was in exactly the same situation. After I had explained this tip, the salesman went to the customer and asked 'if they were given an agency how much business would they do?' The sum was high enough that the salesman agreed to give them an agency. The customer immediately placed a stock order for more than the other agent had sold in the previous year.

Always investigate the conditions under which you would do business. A customer asks, 'Do you make something like this?' Rather than saying 'No', ask how many they need, what they need it for and so on. You may just find a new product line for your company.

Practical Tip No 56

Control

Salespeople often tell me that they like to be in control with a prospect. I think this is much the same as when I was learning to ride a horse. The teacher said to me, 'You have to show the horse who's in control'. My response was, 'That is exactly the problem – the horse has already worked out who's in control!' Unfortunately it wasn't me!

I think customers have worked out who's in control. The money that you are looking for is in their pocket. Nigerian email scams apart, I think if you want to get their money you need to be subtle rather than in control.

A subtle technique that you can use is simply to ask questions and take notes. It is said the person with the pen is in control of a meeting. Check out the minutes of the last meeting you attended!

The effectiveness of asking questions for control is especially evident in getting past 'gatekeepers'.

You are calling on Joe Bloggs, the MD of Acme Products Ltd. His secretary answers. Her job is naturally to screen out people and prevent them from talking to Mr Bloggs.

Typically, the salesperson asks if she can speak with Mr Bloggs and then hands the control to the secretary. She will then be asked:

'Who's calling?' ... 'From which company?' ... 'What is it in connection with?'

The control is with the secretary.

If you end all answers with a question, you have more chance of getting through.

'Who's calling?'
'David Yule. Is he in his office?'
'From which company?'
'GTi Training. Is he available at the moment?'
'What is it in connection with?'

149

You could answer here that you were asked to give him a call (by your chairman or their competitor if asked). My favourite response is, 'I wanted to arrange a meeting with him to discuss new developments in the field of ... or future business strategies in the field of ... Does he control his own diary or can I arrange that with you?'

Never mention free offers etc. They annoy the secretary! You are not trying to sell to the gatekeeper, you are trying to sell the idea that it is beneficial for your target to speak to you.

This tip of using questions is especially important near the end of a sale. After presenting your product or handling an objection, always end with a question. You never want to be in the situation that the prospect is thinking, 'What do they want me to do now?' Always ask the prospect for some activity.

Practical Tip No 57

Control, Influence and Concern

When training, I ask groups to imagine I have just been promoted to Sales Director for their company. I have gathered together this group of expert salespeople and asked them for help. My task is to increase sales. I wouldn't discount anything on the basis of limited budgets. All ideas would be considered. I pose the question 'What could you do to increase sales?'

The list usually includes the following

Ways to increase sales
More Advertising (this almost always comes first)
TV advertising
Newspaper and magazines
Trade shows and publications
Sponsorship
New product lines
Improve existing products
Increase stock
Increase number of salespeople
Increase number of locations
Take over the competition (unlimited budget remember)
Reduce prices
Better cars for salespeople
Incentives
More training (I like to end on a high note!)

Generally these are the answers I get in Europe. I have to say that in Australia, where I think they are more entrepreneurial, the list is often quite different.

I then go on to explain the *Control, Influence and Concern* model. This is based on the model from Stephen Covey's *Seven Habits of*

151

Highly Successful People although I draw different messages and conclusions.

There are things that happen in the world that are completely outside our control. Nothing I do as an individual will ever stop them or change them. I could perhaps motivate others to join me in my cause and that may have an impact but not on my own. I, as an individual, have absolutely no influence over them. I am thinking here about things like poverty, climate change, the economy, crime and so on. They concern me but I have no control or even influence over them.

People who focus their attention on these things get very depressed. If you talk to someone about depression, their focus is a lack of control. They even see their own behaviour and attitude as being completely outside their control.

There are some things that I *can* influence but I still can't control. For example, I can influence customers and colleagues. People who focus on things they can influence are negative and cynical. Their focus is on what other people should be doing. If the customers behaved differently, showed some loyalty, weren't so price conscious and so on …

I believe there is something I have complete, 100% control, over. That is my own attitude. I have found the people in life that are successful and happy focus on this.

Life is 1% what happens to you and 99% how you choose to respond.

When something negative happens, positive people respond in a different way. They don't think about what has happened. They think about what they can do about it.

Look back at the list of 'ways to increase sales' above. When I asked 'what can you do to increase sales?' The average person focuses, not on what they can do, but on what others could do.

For the most part, people in the room have absolutely no control over things on the list. Their influence on these things is nominal. I worked with a Marketing Manager in Romania and he hit the nail on the head. He said, 'We have 100,000 product lines and if I listened to

87 Practical Tips for Dynamic Selling

salespeople I need 100,001. Why do some salespeople focus on the products they don't have rather than sell the ones they do?'

Sacking a salesperson is not the most pleasant job. The only way I could live with it is to believe it was their attitude and behaviour that sacked them. I just brought them the bad news! Maybe in a book I should call it 'letting them go' but I prefer to call a spade a small shovel.

If you ever have had to sack a salesperson, they will blame things that are outside their control. They will say 'the competition is too fierce', even though others are succeeding against the same competition. 'The prices are too high', even though others sell at the same price. The nearest they ever get to self responsibility is to blame their own personality as if it were something they could not control.

Listen to the negative people in your organisation. All their conversation will be about what they can influence rather than what they can control. I saw a presentation by a guy called Larry Winget who invented one of the best sayings I have come across. 'Shut up, stop whingeing and get a life!'

When people are asked about an increase in sales, they could think about what *they* can do. My list goes something like:

> Pick up the phone more times
> Work harder
> See more people
> Ask all of them to buy
> Learn about my own product
> Support my colleagues
> Learn about selling
> Read books about selling (you have made a good start, and I like to end on a high note!)

When I said the answers in Australia were different, their answers were much more like the second list than the first.

Successful salespeople always focus their attention on what they can do. Do your job well before trying to work out how others could do theirs better.

One of the problems in business today is the number of people

87 Practical Tips for Dynamic Selling

who seem to be trying to improve everyone else.

For example, because of the research on the importance of customer service, manufacturers are focussing on getting customer service right. Their focus needs to be on getting their own products right.

The most successful industries as far as I am concerned are the ones where the retailer controls the manufacturer. In the UK, I see many examples of the opposite happening.

Consider the car industry. They will start to get their act together when the big supermarkets enter the market place. The big supermarkets wouldn't put up with the quality problems car dealers have to put up with. According to a JD Power survey, the average new car has four defects when sold to the customer.

Retailers need to be able to reject poor quality easily. It will only happen when manufacturers focus on manufacturing.

Some people make it happen, some happen to make it and some wonder what the hell is happening!

Focus on what you *can* control – what you can do rather than what other people could do. You will be more successful as a result.

Practical Tip No 58

Comparison Theory

Comparison Theory states that we never judge things in isolation – we compare everything with other things and, more importantly, with recent experiences.

For example, try this experiment.

Fill 3 buckets with water, one with hot water, one with really cold water and one with room temperature water.

Put one of your hands in the hot water and at the same time put your other hand in the cold water. Keep them there for a few minutes.

Take both hands out and at the same time plunge them both into the room temperature water. You will experience the odd sensation that one hand will feel that the water is quite warm whilst the other feels that the water is very cold. That is comparison theory at work.

Another experiment you could try is asking people to judge the weight of an object.

Take three objects, one weighing 1 kilo, one weighing 2 kilos and a third weighing 3 kilos.

Give some people the 3 kilo weight, without telling them the weight. Ask them to hold for it one minute and then give them the 2 kilo weight and ask them to guess how much it weighs.

Do the same with another group but this time give them the one kilo weight to hold for one minute then the 2 kilo weight to guess what the weight is. You will find on average the people hold the heavy weight first will consistently estimate the 2 kilo weight as lighter than the group who hold the 1 kilo weight first.

What does this mean for selling? Two things:

- First, you should never mention a price without first mentioning a higher price. The higher price must always be in the same region

155

87 Practical Tips for Dynamic Selling

as the actual price otherwise this technique can work against you.
- Second, you should use *Top Down Selling* (see tip no 60)

Some examples of the use of comparison theory:

Someone telephones you to ask the current price of your fastest selling product. You could answer, 'I think it is £60 – let me check ... no it is actually £57 now.' Note that it has to be in the region or this can actually work against you. If you said, 'I think it is £352 ... no it is actually £24', it would work against you. This is because you are obviously using a technique.

Many direct salespeople selling double glazing, kitchens or conservatories have used a technique called *price conditioning* which uses comparison theory. I have included this merely as an explanation of comparison theory rather than advocating its use.

To explain **price conditioning,** let me take an example of someone selling a kitchen.

> The salesman turns up for the appointment at the prospect's home. After sitting and doing some 'warm up' conversation, he asks about the prospect's thoughts about a kitchen.
>
> He asks them if they have a budget – the prospect says 'No' (see tip 27 – *Budgets*). After having a quick look at the kitchen and being very experienced, the 'designer' knows that for the solid wooden kitchen the prospect mentioned earlier, they are probably looking at £8,000.
>
> Then the salesperson price conditions them to £10,000. It is done by mentioning the sum £10,000 as many times as possible in the presentation. Innocently of course, never connecting directly the £10,000 as the cost of their kitchen.
>
> Some of the things they may say are:
>
> 'The average cost of a wooden kitchen is £10,000.'
>
> 'Look at the quality of these hinges – if you are spending around £10,000, you would expect the hinges to be top quality wouldn't you?'
>
> 'Have you thought of finance?' Everybody answers they will pay cash to this question. 'Aha, so you are the type of person who keeps 10 grand under the bed are you? Even if you do have £10,000 under the bed, I would like to give you an idea of how our finance package would make it

156

87 Practical Tips for Dynamic Selling

easier for you.' Then he sells the benefits of using his own in-house finance package.

He illustrates the finance costs saying, 'I don't know how much your kitchen will cost but say you were borrowing £10,000, which is an easy figure to use'

All the time his objective is solely to mention £10,000 as often as possible.

When he prices up the kitchen at £8,500, mentally the prospect feels she has saved £1,500. Then he does a 'drop close'. 'If you sign on the night, you can get it for £8000.'

You probably wouldn't believe that anyone could be so gullible. It doesn't work every time but I assure you it does work.

When giving prices, you should also use comparison theory. Always compare usual price, retail price, normal price, or some other price so that the final price seems to be lower.

You can use other products as well, for example, saying the Kodak is £500 and the Xerox is only £471.

For some items, using comparison theory is the only way that you can, legitimately use the word 'only'. It is difficult to say this gold plated mobile telephone is only £3,000!! You can however say that this mobile phone was £3,500 and now is only £3,000.

Comparison theory can also be used with a time objection. The customer wants it now but you don't have it in stock and it will take three weeks to get it here.

Compare the three weeks with how long they have been without the product and how long they will keep the product. They keep the product for 10 years, so is it worth rushing and taking a product that isn't exactly what they want? How long have they lived without the product? Another few weeks won't hurt will it?

Another technique using comparison theory is the sticker shocker. In this, when someone asks the price, you inflate the price hugely and very quickly laugh and then tell them the real price. For example, the prospect asks, 'How much is this bath?' The response is, '£2,000 – no that's the total price including the cost of cleaning it and all the water you will use over the next 20 years – ha ha!' Obviously this works better if you make up better jokes!

Practical Tip No 59

Quality v Price

We think as human beings that we judge the quality of an item and then we judge how much it should cost. In other words, when we look at products, we will decide whether we like the item and whether it is made from quality materials ad so on, and then decide whether it is worth the price. In fact, we do exactly the opposite. We use the price to decide on the quality of the item.

It isn't possible to go through life as an amateur scientist analysing every purchase, all the pros and cons of each product, and come to a logical decision on the 'best' purchase. If major purchases were all made in a logical fashion, then there would probably be only one product manufactured in each class – the best. The best product would win.

Some people do try to analyse the pros and cons of products and, as a salesman, I was delighted to find this type of customer.

Imagine customers who are trying to buy a car (I am imagining here because I have never sold cars!). They draw up a big spreadsheet. In column 1 goes the Miles per Gallon (mpg). In column 2 the 0-60 acceleration. Column 3 has the Power to Weight ratio, and so it goes on. At the end, there is a very big spreadsheet with lots of columns.

Try this for yourself and see what happens. You will end up more confused about the decision you want to make. Hence the reason I was delighted to find this type of prospect. They are screaming out for some professional expertise and advice. They just want to know what is the best.

The confusion is because of the way manufacturers choose to describe items. A little different terminology here, a little poetic licence there. Your spreadsheet will have some blank sections and some notes to items in the columns because they are not described in exactly the same way as other manufacturers.

Motor magazines try to do the analysis for you. They consider all

87 Practical Tips for Dynamic Selling

aspects of cars and even then the conclusion almost always comes down to an emotional feel about what is best. It is extremely difficult to differentiate between products in today's market place.

Because it is difficult to determine what is the best quality product, people use the price as an indicator of the quality. It can be a good indicator. Often the best product will cost more. The difficulty is that once understood, it can be, and is being, exploited.

For the most part, if you remove price tags, people would find it difficult to determine quality.

Think about this from a sales perspective. If people judge the quality of an item by the price, then when anything is not selling, it could be because the price is too low.

On courses, I almost always get a story from someone who has tried to sell something and couldn't. They then increased the price and sold the item with no difficulty. I have had stories of houses, tractors, cars where increasing the prices had a positive impact.

One business I worked with was quite sceptical about this. After our training, they took their lowest selling product and increased the price. Within three months it had become their highest selling item.

When I was working in Australia, I spent a fantastic day out with a couple called Phil and Michelle. First Phil flew my wife and myself in his helicopter along the Gold Coast to show us manta ray fish, sharks and kangaroos. They then took us out in their yacht which was moored at the bottom of the garden of their fantastic house (mansion really). I asked Phil about his career.

Phil and Michelle bought a company. I will leave out identifying details because I don't want the market to be aware of the strategy.

The main product of this company sold for $99 Australian. Because it wasn't selling well, Phil decided to reduce the price to $79. The sales were very static.

One day he decided he would try to sell in a slightly more upmarket setting and hiked the price up to $299. He put the product in a box that looked like the product should cost $500. He also gave a two-year guarantee even though competitive products only gave a one-year.

159

87 *Practical Tips for Dynamic Selling*

Was this strategy successful? The helicopter, yacht and mansion should give a clue!

Because of the price, packaging and guarantee, customers perceived the quality to be higher.

The tip here is – if something isn't selling, then increase the price. It is as likely to be not selling because it is being perceived as low quality rather than not selling because the price is too high. If this fails, you can always bring the price down again to the original price and show it as a 'sale' item, using greed to sell it.

Practical Tip No 60

Top-down Selling

Most sales people find themselves describing a range of products at some time. The customer has said, 'I don't know what I want, what do you have?'

One of the fabulous techniques of the Owl (see tip no 39 – *Behaviour*) is to get you answering your own questions. Often with an Owl you will find yourself presenting a range of products and describing the differences between them.

I came across an experiment conducted in Australia (I am sorry I have forgotten the source) and since then have used this technique successfully many times. The success is due mainly to the operation of Comparison Theory.

In the experiment there were two sales teams. Whenever they presented a range of products, the first team were asked to present them starting at the bottom of the range, for example:

- 'This is the *entry level* model (basic model, beginners etc.) ...
- next we have the intermediate range ...
- finally we have the *top of the range*.'

In other words to sell from the bottom up.

The second sales team was asked to do exactly the opposite. They were asked to present products from the top down, for example:

- 'Let me show you the top of the range – it has these features and these benefits ...
- then we have the intermediate range – it doesn't have xyz ...
- and finally we have the lower range and it doesn't have (or only has) xyz.

The second team that sold from the top down outsold the first team by over 40%.

161

87 Practical Tips for Dynamic Selling

Let me explain why I think this happened.

First of all, during the experiment, the first team (selling bottom-up) didn't sell a single top range product. The second team (selling top-down) didn't sell a single bottom range product.

If you start from the bottom up, the prospect stops you when you reach the level they want to buy and therefore you often don't present the top of the range. The same happens with top down but they stop you at a higher level and you always get the opportunity to present the top of the range.

Comparison theory says we somehow feel that if we have been talking about something that costs £3,000, by the time we get to the bottom of the range, £500 sounds like nothing.

We don't like to lose things we have already got and so the presentation of saying 'the intermediate doesn't have' sounds like you are taking things away from them.

We use the price to judge the quality (see tip no 59)

When people are buying to avoid loss, they are more speculative (see tip no 77 – *Decision Making*) and top down means when it is broken to the ridiculous (see tip no 74), then the difference in cost is negligible.

What I find remarkable about top-down selling is I have never met anyone that did this naturally. I have met people that are trained to do top-down Selling but never naturally. Cosmetic salespeople are always taught that when someone asks for perfume, you always get the large bottle. It is easier to sell a smaller size if that isn't acceptable.

When giving a range of prices, almost everybody I know does it from the bottom up. We sell houses from £100,000 upwards. Our products start at £1,000 up to £3,000 and so on.

Because of the research on Comparison Theory, I think a new trend is happening. Restaurant wine lists are no longer being shown from lowest price to highest. I have noticed a few car adverts that are bucking the trend as well by going from the top down.

I think it seems intuitively easier to explain the bottom of the range and the features than it does starting with the top.

Try top-down Selling and see what it does for your sales figures.

Terminology

Just a word on the terminology. I have worked with companies that describe their range as entry level or basic level. No prospect wants to hear this terminology and so, unless you are deliberately trying to talk them out of buying one, try to find other ways to describe it.

One company I worked with described their range as Good, Better and Best. They have products that they say are good quality. A mid range that is better quality and a top range that is best quality.

Other terms you may use are:

Luxury, comfort, value for money

Rolls Royce, BMW and Ford

I am sure there are many other creative ways of doing this.

Spin-offs

If you use top-down selling there are a couple of spin-offs.

You don't have to ask for a budget. What you will find is that people will tend to dislike items that are over their budget and tend to prefer products they feel they can afford. Say, for example, you are selling televisions. You go to the top of the range Bang & Olfsen and present it. People who feel it is over their budget will have a tendency to dislike the style. Too modern, too sleek or whatever.

You keep going down and show the television at £3,000, they don't like that one either. Then the television at £2,000 – they like this one!

Many salespeople have said to me they feel there is a danger in top-down selling. The customer tells you they are shopping around and were thinking of a certain product or perhaps they say the have a budget of £1,000. You know the product they're thinking of is a mid-range product costing £1,000.

If you start off by presenting a product costing £3,000, isn't there a danger of having people feel you are very expensive and also inattentive to their needs.

Clearly this is a possibility worthy of attention and in these circumstances you may wish to consider:

1. that you are making a negative assumption that they won't buy or can't afford a better product

87 Practical Tips for Dynamic Selling

2. that you could still mention it even if you feel really uncomfortable, e.g. you could say, 'There probably isn't any point of showing you the top of the range £3,000 model then, is there?'

I would still start with a product more expensive than £1,000. I consider £1,000 to be a minimum not a maximum.

If you use top-down selling and the price is over their budget. You will find the discussion naturally tends to go towards looking at less expensive products rather than lowering the price. This works in the same way as using a ballpark figure (tip no 46).

If you ask for a budget and the price goes over their budget, the discussion tends to be about reducing the price rather than changing the spec.

I have also been asked about the concept of *good, better, best*. Do I mean price or quality? For example, let's say there are three DVD recorders. One at £200, one at £300 and one costing £500? The salesperson thinks the one at £300 is the best quality. Which is good, which better and which best?

You need to distinguish between *presenting* and *giving your opinion*. When presenting, I only use price to describe the categories good, better, best. In the DVD example, £200 is good, £300 better and £500 is best. If I am giving my opinion, that is different.

First of all only give your opinion to people who would consider it worthy. That means Doves (at any time) and Peacocks or Owls (only if asked for it). (see tip no 39 – *Deal with the Behaviour*).

If you are giving your opinion, you should also use the word 'because' in the sentence (see tip no 8).

Practical Tip No 61

Present Your Products in the Right Order

When talking about top-down selling, how should you display products? Paco Underhill in his great book '*Why We Buy*' gives a full insight as to how and where products should be displayed.

Top-down selling and comparison theory would say that you need to tailor this to your individual business.

I have already said that when entering a show-room, people normally turn left and most stop at the same place (see tip no 16 – *Approach in the Right Way*). That suggests your highest priced item should be placed there. As people go round clockwise, so the price should go top down.

On a rack, because of the way we read, the top seller should be the eye catching product. It should go in the middle with the highest priced just to the right of it and the lowest price to the left:

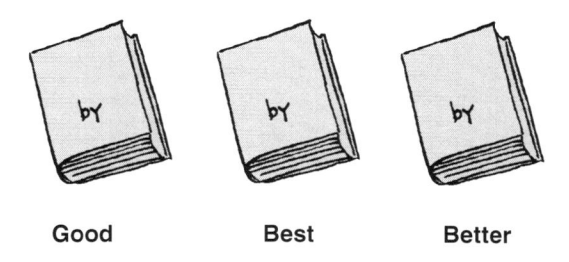

Good   **Best**   **Better**

You really need to study your environment and work out which way is most effective for you.

Practical Tip No 62

The Power of One

When presenting proposals, always use **one per cent** difference.

One per cent is a powerful number because it seems easily achievable.

Take 1% for a big organisation, BT for example. If my selling tips could improve the performance of their sales team by just one per cent!

Their turnover is	£18,519,000,000
A one per cent increase would be	£185,190,000

Yes that's right – **ONE HUNDRED AND EIGHTY-FIVE MILLION, ONE HUNDRED AND NINETY THOUSAND POUNDS**!!!

But their costs would only change marginally (let say the cost of this book!!!) That would add, for the sake of this example, £180 million to their profit.

Their actual profit was a mere   £ 1,948,000,000

They could have added nearly 10% to their bottom line, just with a 1% improvement in sales.

1% always seems achievable and realistic to people, yet when it is related back to profit it is quite unbelievable!

I have had some phenomenal results with clients by looking for 1% here and there.

Practical Tip No 63

Testimonials

I have never used testimonials. If I am asked about other companies I work with, I will disclose the industries of clients I have worked with. I can also talk about the size of the companies. I am giving a strategy to gain a competitive advantage and I never disclose the names of clients I work with. You never know whom you are talking to.

I do give an undertaking that I will never talk about any other client's business with them and I will never talk about them to other clients. I will also undertake not to work with any of their direct competitors. I have never lost any business by refusing to disclose clients.

That apart, some companies do use testimonials and letters of recommendations.

If you do, then try to use testimonials that have one uncomplimentary remark. They are much more believable and trusted than letters which say you are the best thing since sliced bread and you never make mistakes.

Remarks such as, 'the delivery was a little late but you pulled out all the stops for me and I appreciate it', are more believable.

Practical Tip No 64

Avoid pain

A psychologist (Kahneman) had a fascinating finding that, everything else being equal, most people are much more interested in making sure they don't lose money than they are in actually making any. When we mentally balance the books, we put more weight on the value of a loss, giving it two to three times the importance we give to the value of the size of gain. This has been confirmed in hundreds of subsequent experiments.

People buy products for three reasons:

- habit
- emotion or
- logic

Of the emotions, fear and greed are the most important. Most marketing strategies try to combine fear with greed, e.g. 'Special rate offer ends soon!'

Cialdini tells a wonderful story about using greed to sell.

> Two brothers have a tailoring business. One brother is a little deaf. When serving, he is always asking the customers to repeat themselves because he is hard of hearing. The customer seems to be interested in a blue suit and has asked the price. The 'deaf' brother shouts to the other one, 'Bob, how much is this blue suit?'
>
> The answer comes back, '$70' (suits are obviously much cheaper in America!)
>
> 'How much did you say – $50?
>
> '$70' (said a little louder).
>
> He turns to the customer and says, 'Bob says the suit is $50'. People buy the suit and are out of the shop as quickly as possible before the 'deaf' brother discovers his 'mistake'.

87 Practical Tips for Dynamic Selling

An example of how people are more motivated by fear than greed is people who quit smoking. The people who try to stop smoking because of the pleasure it will give are not particularly successful. I am sure everyone knows someone that has tried to stop and failed. Contrast that with the success of people who are told they have some terrible disease and they must give up. Alcohol, George Best apart!, has the same effect.

If this is so, all sales presentations should be geared towards highlighting the current or projected pain and how your product would remove the pain.

This changes your questioning style from finding out needs to looking for pain. What hurts the company? How do they lose money? When things go wrong, what happens and what do they have to do to put it right?

I was working with a distributor recently and we discussed this. As a test one of the regional managers went out the very next day and asked his major clients. He reckoned he got to understand more about their buying motivation in one meeting than he had in ten years of dealing with the client.

One other thing will happen if you look for pain. If you ask a prospect, 'What do we need to do to get your business?' The most popular answer is 'low price'. Despite this we know that low price is not a motivator to buy.

Ask prospects about pain – 'how do they lose money on contracts?' I have never had anyone say my prices cause them to lose money. Looking for pain removes a discussion away from how low can you get your price. The focus comes away from price altogether to service and product quality issues.

Often salespeople will tell me that business-to-business is more price sensitive than retail. I don't believe this to be true. I believe the perception arises because of the way most salespeople approach selling in a business-to-business environment.

In retail sales, customers have to pay for the goods themselves.

In business sales, the trader charges the end customer. They add a percentage on top of your price to the end user. How much you charge them is largely irrelevant since they are simply charging the cost on. The business customer is focused (or should be by the salesperson) on profit not price. In fact, because they add a percentage, they make more money with higher prices!

What concerns business customers more is making a profit from their purchase. When you talk to them about losing money, the factors that cost them money are usually concerning late deliveries, broken promises, damaged goods, faulty goods, rework and so on.

Practical Tip No 65

Sell 'Through People'

The first time I heard this expression was from the owner of a company that makes watches. He sold *through* jewellers.

He had recognised that, because he was selling speciality watches, he didn't have to sell the watch to the dealer. He had to teach the jeweller to sell the watches to the consumer. He was trying to sell to the end consumer 'through' the jeweller.

This applies to most selling. The retail example above, using watches, is obvious. In business-to-business selling I realised that if the *technical buyer* approved a product but the *user buyer* didn't the users would win. (See tip no 12 – *Sell what is personally important*) You have to sell through User buyers to Technical buyers, and through Technical buyers to Economic buyers.

In order to get repeat sales for a product, you have to learn to sell through people. Your focus has to be how to get the end users to approve.

Practical Tip No 66

When to Sell Accessories

Accessories have to be pitched at the right time to be sold effectively.

To decide the right time, you need to decide whether the accessory enhances or protects the purchase.

For example, when you go to a restaurant, wine enhances a meal, so they have to sell wine at the beginning or during – never after. Leave suggesting a glass of port too long after the meal has finished and you have lost your chance.

Indigestion tablets are protectors. They have to be sold after the meal!

For example, if you are selling a car, a stereo system enhances the purchase. You need to build up the desire for a stereo system during the sale. After it has been concluded is too late. If you are selling a 5-year full service warranty, you should wait until after you have agreed the sale.

After you have made the sale, you can make use of comparison theory (tip no 58) to make the additional sum insignificant.

'Now I assume you will (+ve) want to protect your £30,000 investment in a car, won't (-ve) you!' This makes use of Positive followed by a negative (see tip no 33)

Practical Tip No 67

Don't Do What Others Do

Try to avoid doing what every other salesperson does.

I bet your company sells based on the quality of the product and the quality of the service. You acknowledge you are not the lowest price in the market.

What do you think your competitors are saying?

'Our products are crap and we keep screwing up on the service but at least we have the cheapest prices!'

The reason I could make my bet confidently is I have yet to come across the company that does sell by the second method. Everybody claims to have good quality and good service.

If there is one rule in selling it should be not to do what everybody else does. When I was taught to sell, I was taught many different closing techniques (see tip no 81). One of them was the alternative close. My friend, who is not and never has been a salesman, said when it is used on him he feels like screaming. When the layman starts to recognise the techniques then it is time to stop.

You should never tell people what techniques you use on them.

I also never tell a salesperson that he or she could have got more money out of me! You know the scenario, you want to buy something and the salesperson makes a final offer. You say unless they come down to £xx, you won't buy. As you are walking out, the salesperson calls you back and says, 'Okay, you are a hard man but I will match your price'. As they are writing up the order, they ask if you would have come back and bought it at the higher price. Never tell them you would have. What a way to destroy someone!!

Practical Tip No 68

Objections

The only reason companies employ salespeople is because there are objections. If there were no objections, there wouldn't be any need for salespeople. Once informed of the product, customers would buy and continue to buy. The marketing function would be supreme (as happens with many high branded 'fashion items' e.g. Nike)

As a salesperson, your only function is to handle objections. Most objections you handle before they occur in your presentation. That is the purpose of a presentation, helping the prospect to avoid the objections – 'I don't need it' or 'It isn't worth it' and so on.

It is far more successful to handle objections before they occur rather than after they occur! This is because there are several things at play with objections:

Why? (tip no 6)
The most obvious answer to any objection and the one you are almost pre-programmed to ask is 'Why?' Imagine a prospect said to you, 'I don't like the colour/design/style/feature etc.' You will probably recognise that you are itching to ask 'why?' We do this to try to find out what they do like and yet all you find out is their justification for this statement. Try focusing on what they do like, e.g. 'What would the perfect product be like/do for you etc.'

People don't like to be proved wrong (tip no 19)
This means that whatever happens in the objection, if you make it into an 'us v you' situation, you are almost bound to fail. When I was taught to sell, I was taught that when someone objected, you pointed out other advantages. For example, the prospect said, 'It is too expensive' and you said, 'Yes, but it is better quality because of …' The prospect said, 'I don't like the design' and you said, 'Yes, but it does tuck away in a corner and so it will be out of sight' and so on.

174

(See tip no 69 – *The 3rd Most Powerful Word in Selling*). This is not highly successful because people don't like to be proved wrong.

I saw an obvious example of this with a salesperson trying to sell a Makita drill rather than a Black & Decker. The following conversation actually took place:

Customer: 'I think the Makita is too expensive for me.'
Salesperson: Yes, I understand it costs more but the Makita is better quality.'
Customer: 'Yes, but I do rough jobs that are out of sight and I don't need the holes to look perfect.'
Salesperson: 'Yes, but the drill will last longer and cost you less in the long term.'
Customer: 'Yes, but this is only the second drill I have ever bought and I don't need it to last long.'
Salesperson: 'Yes, but if you are drilling into heavy materials, this one won't burn out.'
Customer: 'Yes, but it will probably be nicked because it is better!'
... and so on.

Confirmation bias (tip no 3)

Customers seek evidence to prove what they believe and that they are right and will be prepared to ignore any evidence you may show to the contrary. This means how you handle the objection is critical using their beliefs rather than yours.

Control, influence and concern (tip no 57)

You have to focus on things within your control. No one ever sells to everyone and I wish salespeople would recognise this. Stop trying to sell to everyone. Go on a voyage of discovery with the customer and see if you can make a convincing argument that would convince YOU to buy the product before trying to convince the customer!

Reciprocity (tip no 41)

Concessions are generally met with concessions. If you fight the customers, they will fight you. Hence all the arguments above which use 'yes...but' in every sentence.

Correlations (tip no 36)

There is a strong correlation between objections and sales.

Objections are not questions – they are statements. 'That is too expensive' is not a question. 'I don't like it' isn't a question. 'Do you deliver on a Wednesday?' is a question – not an objection. Having said that, it helps when hearing an objection to think of the question that is behind the objection.

Whenever you hear an objection, try thinking what it really means.

Humans rarely ask the right question. For example if I say to my wife, 'Are you going into the kitchen?', the real question is probably 'Would you make me a cup of tea!'

If I ask, 'Do you have £20?', the real question is probably, 'How prepared are you to lend or give me £20!'

When you hear an objection, try to think of the real question. For example, 'I can buy it cheaper elsewhere' is probably, 'What difference is there between this product/your service that makes you feel the extra is worth it?'

In handling objections, the first thing that needs to be accepted is that I don't have any arguments against the objection. To take an example – if your customer says your product is too expensive because they can buy it cheaper elsewhere, I have no arguments against this statement. I don't know if they really can get the same product elsewhere (a little on this later). I also don't know how your service compares with 'elsewhere'. I therefore have no knowledge of you, your competitors, your products, your services etc on which to base any arguments.

In my experience, thinking about arguments is the least of your problems. I have never had a salesperson that couldn't think of arguments. The problem was simply that the customers wouldn't accept the arguments.

If the customers accepted your arguments, then the problem would be solved. The customer would say, 'You are too expensive because I can buy it cheaper down the road'. You would answer, 'Yes, but our service is better than theirs, or our product is better quality than theirs'. If they accepted these arguments, they would say, 'Oh is it? Really? Well thank you for that – I had better buy from you then – here is my money!'

87 Practical Tips for Dynamic Selling

Have you ever noticed the really annoying thing about objections? Unfortunately, the customers don't always accept your arguments. I have even seen examples of customers appearing to accept the argument – 'I agree that yours is better quality but I am still going to buy elsewhere!'

The only thing I can help you with is I that have a method that helps people listen to and be more willing to accept your arguments.

The stages are:

- **STFU**
- **Empathy Statement**
- **Handle**
- **Close**
- **STFU**

STFU stands for 'Stop Talking!' (Shut the folder up!)

The first thing you need to do when you hear an objection is to use the one-second rule (see tip no 29).

Let's take the objection, 'That is too expensive'

Imagine someone has just said that to you. What might they mean by this statement?

I can think of:

- ✘ The product isn't worth the price.
- ✘ There is another product that is less expensive.
- ✘ It is a higher cost than I expected.
- ✘ It isn't worth that much more than another similar product (e.g. a Skoda compared with a Ford).
- ✘ They can't afford it.
- ✘ It is too good quality (e.g. a Rolls Royce is too expensive for me).
- ✘ Someone told them they should pay less than that amount.
- ✘ It could be the start of a negotiation strategy.
- ✘ They don't like it.

I think before you even attempt to handle the objection, you should find out what they mean by 'too expensive'.

Note here that the most natural thing here would be to ask them,

177

'Why do you think it is too expensive?' or 'What makes you say that?' or 'How come?' The second two are infinitely preferable to the first one because of the power of the word 'why' (see tip no 6). None of these ways is brilliant however.

All of them involve your forcing the prospect to take a stand and because they don't want to be proved wrong (see tip no 19), you actually make it harder for them to back down.

The one-second rule (tip no 29) is a perfect strategy here. That is because of a concept known as *'Preferred responses and Non Preferred Responses'*.

When people give you a preferred response, they do not feel the need to explain. When people give you a non-preferred response, they always feel the need to explain.

For example, if you ask someone if they would like a cup of tea, people will be able to say 'yes please' without giving an explanation. If they want to say 'No', that is a non-preferred response and they will always feel the need to explain.

This means that you only have to listen carefully and not speak for one second to hear the explanation.

They will say things such as:
'No thanks, I've just had one,'
'No thanks, I'm in a hurry,'
'No thanks, I don't like tea,' ... and so on

All objections are, by definition, 'non-preferred responses'

If prospects say that is too expensive and you leave them a one-second gap, they will explain and tell you what exactly they mean.

Only when you have an explanation – a full understanding of the objection – can you hope to handle it.

This takes us on to the next stage:

Empathy Statements

The customers expectations are critical at this stage. Imagine if you were being sold a chair and you said to the salesperson that you 'thought the chair was too expensive ... it isn't good quality'. What would you expect the salesperson to do? Most of us would expect the

87 Practical Tips for Dynamic Selling

salesperson to show the quality of the manufacture and show us how we were wrong. In essence we expect salespeople to argue with us!

Because of this expectation, we are resistant to any arguments from the salesperson at this time.

If you want people to listen to your arguments, you need to construct an empathy statement. Here is the difficult part – an empathy statement cannot include the words 'but' 'however' or 'although' at any time. Nor can they include the phrase 'on the other hand' or similar. These are arguments – not empathy statements.

An Empathy Statement should always end with a positive followed by a negative (see tip no 33) Examples are, don't we, shouldn't we etc.

Examples of empathy statements are included in the next tip.

The word 'but' is the 3rd most powerful word and deserves a tip all of its own! (see tip no 69).

The third stage of handling objections is:

Handle

Okay now you get to put your superior knowledge of the product, competitors and your service.

Some strategies for handling objections are:
- Break it to the ridiculous (tip no 74).
- Is it the cost or the price that you are concerned with? (tip no 75).
- Use humour.
  If I am asked for my best price (a question – not an objection) I use humour. For example, if I am selling something at £300 and I am asked if it is my best price, I respond, 'No, I could do it for £400 but it is best for me, unfortunately.' You would be amazed how often this works.
- Get them to sell the product to you (tip no 71).

Close

Every time you handle an objection you should end up with a question (see tip no 56). This will reduce the number of objections you get.

STFU (again)

179

Practical Tip No 69

The Third Most Powerful Word in Selling

An empathy statement cannot include the word 'but'. Any sentence including 'but' at this time is not an empathy statement – it is an argument.

It is very difficult to avoid an argument with someone who keeps using the word 'but'. It is also very difficult to argue with someone that never uses the word 'but'.

In order to avoid saying the word 'but', people substitute 'however' or 'although'. These have the same effect as 'but'. They convert an empathy statement into an argument, and they are slightly more palatable. If you can construct a proper empathy statement, you will get into fewer arguments.

Of all the tips I am giving in this book I think this one is the hardest to implement. I was speaking at a Sales Conference for a company with hundreds of people in the audience and got a line of participants trying to win a £20 note. All they had to do was go through my exercise without saying the word 'but'. I have never lost my £20 at any conference!

On one occasion, only one spectator in the audience actually heard a participant saying 'but'. I left it for about 10 seconds before the spectator shouted out that the participant had said 'but'.

Almost with one voice, the audience were shouting that the spectator had made a mistake because the participant hadn't said 'but'. It was only when I repeated the sentence he *had* said, that people realised 'but' was used.

It is so ingrained in our language we find it very difficult to handle objections without saying but. On courses, I will let people have some time to think about an empathy statement for the objections we have listed. Even given some time to think about it, some people find it almost impossible.

87 *Practical Tips for Dynamic Selling*

Often people will write an empathy statement and when they read it out, even though they are reading from a piece of paper they still add in 'but'!

The best advice I can give when constructing an empathy statement is to have an open mind. Customers may be right and you should help them to check

So, to construct an empathy statement you should:
1. avoid the word 'but'
2. make it as a statement not a question
3. end with a positive and then negative (see tip no 33 – *Getting to Yes*)
4. say it in a helpful tone rather than an arguing tone.

So an empathy statement for the above objections may be:

The product isn't worth the price.
Yes, I can understand that and what we need to do is look at all the features to see whether it is the correct product for you, don't we.

There is another product that is less expensive.
Yes, I can understand that. There are many cheaper products available in the market place and if I could get exactly the same thing cheaper elsewhere, I would buy it as well. What we need to do is look and check that it is exactly the same, don't we.

It is a higher cost than I expected.
I would use the one-second rule again to see what they want to do about it.

It isn't worth that much more than another similar product (e.g. **a Skoda compared with a Ford).**
Yes, I can see that. They look very similar don't they and what we

need to do is take a close look at the products and see if the differences are worthwhile for you, don't we.

I can't afford it.
I would use the one-second rule again to see what they want to do about it.

It is too good quality (e.g. a Rolls Royce is too expensive for me).
Yes I can understand that and what we need to do is look at all the features to see whether it is the correct product for you, don't we.

Someone told me I should pay less than that amount.
I would use the one-second rule again to see what they want to do about it.

It could be the start of a negotiation strategy, i.e. is that your best price?
Yes I want to make it as attractive as possible and we should investigate any suggestions you have to make our proposal as attractive as possible, shouldn't we. I would then ask them what suggestions they have.

I don't like it.
I would use the one-second rule again to see what they do want.

Practical Tip No 70

Feel, Felt, Found

An example of an empathy statement is the *feel, felt, found* method.

The idea here is to make up a sentence with these three words included. The critical factor is using the word 'and' between the 'felt' and the 'found' parts. People find it more natural to use 'but' and it is more powerful to use 'and'.

Objections and feel, felt, found statements

The product isn't worth the price.
I understand how you feel about that. Many customers have felt the same way and what they found is that when they considered this feature and that feature it was worth paying the additional cost.

There is another product that is less expensive.
I understand how you feel about that, many customers have felt the same way and what they found is that when they bought the cheaper product they ended up replacing it and losing money.

It is a higher cost than I expected.
I understand how you feel about that, many customers have felt the same way and what they found is that when they considered this feature and that feature it was worth paying the additional cost.

It isn't worth that much more than another similar product (e.g. a Skoda compared with a Ford).
You may have noticed the annoying habit that the answers to every objection appear to be almost exactly the same. That is because almost every answer is exactly the same! For this reason

183

87 Practical Tips for Dynamic Selling

you should certainly never use a feel, felt, found more than once with the same person.

I can't afford it.
Construct your own feel, felt, found sentence using the above examples.

It is too good quality (e.g. a Rolls Royce is too expensive for me)
Construct your own feel, felt, found sentence using the above examples.

Practical Tip No 71

Get the Prospect to Sell the Product to You

Case 1

The prospect has objected to the price, saying that it is too expensive. You used the one-second rule and he said, 'Is there any way you can give me a better price?'

You have used an empathy statement and now you want to handle the objection, so get him *to sell the product to you.*

You should say, 'I need to check this is the right product for you.' or, 'Is this the product you are looking for?'

When the prospect confirms it is, ask, 'Why?' (disguising it in the middle of a sentence – see tip no 7)

Everything he says reduces your need to give a discount.

Case 2

Suppose the objection is that you are too expensive. After the one-second rule, he says, 'I can buy it cheaper elsewhere'.

You ask, 'If the price was the same in both places where would you prefer to buy from?'

If he says it is from you (and that should be what he says, otherwise why is he here?).

Ask him why? Everything he says reduces your need to give a discount. You may then use tip no 73 – *Fast Good Cheap* or tip no 75 – *Cost v Price*.

Of course, when you ask where would the prospects prefer to buy from, they could say either that they don't care or that they would prefer to buy from your competitor.

If they don't care, you have to start working on differentiators and

87 Practical Tips for Dynamic Selling

if you can't differentiate between the competitor and yourselves, then you have made price more important. Read tip no 78 – *Four Differentiators*.

If they would prefer to buy from your competitor, you might just be in trouble!! What is vitally important here is that you don't ask them the very question you are itching to ask them. You must never ask them why they would prefer to buy from your competitor, see tip no 6 – *'Why'*. Instead focus on what would be the ideal supplier. What they *do want*, rather than *why they don't want* to buy from you.

Practical Tip No 72

Discounting

My own personal belief is that salespeople should not be allowed to discount. Neither do I appreciate the salesperson running an errand for me to negotiate with their boss. I am a good negotiator. I want to talk to the boss, to do it myself. Bring them out to face me!

In sales, we should sell the product at a given price. Our focus should be on selling the product. Because of discounting, some industries spend more time teaching people discounting strategies than good selling.

I acknowledge that there are some industries where they use price as a reason to buy now. I don't agree that price is a reason to buy – but it is a reason to buy now. It uses fear and greed (see tip no 64 – *Avoid Pain*) to get the sale today.

I agree with set discounts based on quantity. However, they should *be* set. If you buy one, here is the price; if you buy 1,000 there should be a different price because of the economies of scale. The discounts should be fixed. It shouldn't matter whether you are a good negotiator. The only consideration is level of profit.

When talking about discounting, I am not talking about the big sign at the door that says '50% off everything'. These were designed for a specific purpose and they work. They also use fear and greed – '50% off everything. Sale must end soon!'

They were not designed to give discounts but to stop people from asking for a discount. If you have a big sign saying '50% off', fewer people ask for a discount. I worked with an organisation that had an October sale every year (in October as luck would have it!). Their margin increased during the sale. This happened because normally people asked for a discount and the average discount was 10%.

During the sale, the sale price was 8% below the retail price and very few people asked for a further discount. If they did, they were told it was discounted already in the sale, as if that was the end of the matter!

87 Practical Tips for Dynamic Selling

If you use discounting, here are some strategies to help.

The discounts I will give some tips about are the ones negotiated with individual customers. Most would not be given to customers if the discount wasn't asked for.

The first thing to recognise about these is that most discounts are negotiated *after* the decision to buy has been taken. Why would you negotiate on something you don't want? People decide they want something and then negotiate the best price they can get.

There are some problems with these discounts. Would you trust a company that would try to cheat you? Every time a customer asks for a discount and it is given, the message is 'we cheat our customers'. In fact, we would have cheated you as well if you hadn't asked for a discount.

There are some things that increase the feeling of cheating and some that reduce it.

A study showed that the first time a customer starts to think about your profit is when a discount is mentioned.

There are also some signals that sound like a starting point for negotiation. There are some ways that you can make a discount sound like the finishing point in a negotiation. The effect of sounding like a starting point is it encourages people to ask for more. The effect of sounding like a finishing point is it reduces the number of people that ask for more.

Let me give you a scenario. You are buying a carpet and ask for a discount. The salesperson offers you 40% off. What would you be thinking? Chances are you think they must be making a high profit if they can afford to give away that amount. You may also be thinking the carpet is probably not such good quality as you had first thought. With that much margin, the cost of manufacture must be low.

Then you go to buy four new computers for your office. The salesperson offers just 1¼% discount for quantity. This time you are probably thinking these are tight margin products. The sellers probably don't make much profit on them. The are worth the original price and so the quality is supported by the price.

The strange thing is that when we are offered a lower discount, we think the profit is lower and the quality is better.

188

87 Practical Tips for Dynamic Selling

Start with a small percentage
The first rule therefore in discounting is to offer a low percentage.

What if the salesperson offered you the most popular discount in selling? 10% off!

A study showed that people who were given 10% discount after a negotiation were less satisfied than people who were not given any discount. Why might this be?

The reason could be that when they get home, they start to think maybe they could have got more. If only they had been a little more courageous and kept going. Round figures do that for you. They sound too off pat and they sound like a starting point not an ending point.

Use single percentages
Odd percentages seem like they have been calculated specifically for this situation. They sound like an ending point.

Include the number 7 in your final figure
Harvard business school did a study and found that the number seven is a special number for humans. There are 7 wonders of the world, 7 oceans, 7th heaven, lucky 7, 7 days in the week, 7 habits of highly successful people (Stephen Covey).

In the Koran it says if you don't like someone, you should think of 77 reasons for liking them before one reason for disliking them.

Native Americans had a saying that if you don't like someone you should walk 7 miles in their shoes. Then if you still don't like them you are 7 miles away and you have their shoes!

Make the numbers go down at the end
Harvard discovered that the figure £3,761 would be accepted more often than the figure £3,689

This was for two reasons. The first was because the number 7 appears in the first sum. The second reason is that £3,761 is reducing at the end whereas £3,689 is increasing at the end.

Harvard also found that if a negotiation took place from these figures, the one with numbers reducing at the end would retain a higher price.

This is the first research I have ever encountered that challenged the practice of pricing at £19.99 because it sounds less than £20. Marks and Spencers in the UK abandoned the £19.99 pricing and used rounded figures without suffering ill effects. Of course, they have recently had problems for different reasons. £20 still sounds too rounded for me.

Take a long time to calculate the discount

It isn't logical for someone to say to you, 'How much discount can you give me?' and you respond immediately with 8.7963 recurring!

Fortunately I have a solution. When you take longer to calculate a discount people believe it to be a more accurate discount and a finishing point.

Refer to lots of documents

The same goes for the number of documents you refer to when calculating the discount.

Refer to price lists, stock lists etc.

Add a pound every time

The next time you calculate a discount, add back one pound to the final figure after calculating the discount.

I imagine, because you are reading this book, you are a good salesperson. How much business do you think you would lose if you tried this? I don't think you would lose any business.

One organisation I worked with would have increased their profit by more than £1 million if they added just £1 to every invoice. Of course, not all of them involved discounting but even £1 each time can add up to a substantial sum.

Of course, you are probably saying how much business would I lose if I added £2 rather than £1 to the final figure? In all probability you would not lose any business. So, you should use the concept of adding a pound rather than the amount. Add a small figure back in to round up to an odd amount.

87 Practical Tips for Dynamic Selling

Round up to an odd figure

What I found is that salespeople naturally round down when discounting. If your final figure came to £3,689 I am suggesting you should adjust it up to £3,761. I suggest you round up to an odd amount adding as many pounds as you can without losing the business.

In most cases, you don't lose the business if you add too many pounds, you just get asked for more discount!

If you follow these guidelines, you will make more profit and encourage customer loyalty and trust. This is because the discounting strategies prevent people from thinking you are trying to cheat them.

Practical Tip No 73

Fast, Good and Cheap

This is mainly used when a customer has indicated they would prefer to deal with you but your price is higher. You ask them why they would prefer to deal with you and then explain *fast, good and cheap*.

It can also be used when you have a customer who is always complaining about your prices and telling you everyone else has lower prices.

Of the three words 'fast', 'good' and 'cheap', the common law of business states you can only get any two from the three. You are a business person and I am sure you appreciate that. Any company that tries to provide all three has to go out of business.

Which two would you prefer from fast, good and cheap?

Most customers answer fast and good
We do fast and good but it cannot be cheap as well. There is a cost of fast, extra staff, higher stock etc. There is also a cost for 'good' and so you can get fast and good but it can't be cheap.

The next alternative is good and cheap
We can do good and cheap but it isn't fast. You need to wait until I get a cancelled order or the manufacturer adds a support. We do have stock which is good that we want to sell off cheaply from time to time. Would you like me to keep you informed when it is good and cheap?

Finally fast and cheap
This isn't a market we are in. There are lots of companies in the market place providing fast and cheap but it is not good. Ultimately of course it also ends up costing more. (This would naturally lead into *Cost v Price* – see tip no 75.)

Practical Tip No 74

Break It to the Ridiculous

The customer has objected, you have used the one-second rule (tip no 29) and have given an empathy statement (tip no 69). You are now into handling the objection.

A tip here is to break things to the ridiculous.

Imagine you are buying a hi-fi. The one you want costs £500 but you feel that is too expensive. Breaking it to the ridiculous involves handling the objection using the smallest amount possible.

For example, with a £500 hi-fi, the alternative would be to get one that is slightly lower quality which would cost say £400.

What we are talking about is £100 difference.

The average hi-fi today probably lasts for 10 years (I have had my hi-fi for longer than that).

We are now talking about £10 a year or less than £1 per month. That is less than 25p per week or about 3p per day.

Is it worth paying an extra 3p per day to get exactly what you want?

The same technique can be used with time.

Practical Tip No 75

Cost v Price

The customer has objected to the price, you have used the one-second rule (tip no 29) and have given an empathy statement (tip no 69). You are now into handling the objection.

'Is it the cost or price that concerns you?'

The typical answer would be, 'What do you mean?'

Well, the price is the amount you pay in the short term. The cost is how much it costs you in total.

For example, suppose you are a tradesman charging £20 per hour. You buy something for a *price* of £20 and it takes you one hour to drive to the merchants and back. The *cost* to you is £40.

I have always wondered about this with supermarkets. I go to a supermarket to buy groceries. It takes me 30 minutes to drive there. I use a gallon of petrol which costs me £4. I add 40 miles depreciation to the car. I spend 1 hour in the supermarket, 30 minutes to drive back and I save £10 over shopping in the village! Where is the logic in that?

The price is lower but the cost is higher. I use the internet.

If I buy a piece of furniture for £500 and, because it is low quality, I have to replace it in 4 years' time with another at £500, the cost is £1,000 compared with £750 to buy better quality in the first place.

When I use this technique, I would always use it with some of the following value quotations.

'Buying cheap can cost you dearly.'

'You only get what you pay for.'

'The bitterness of poor quality lingers long after the sweet taste of low price is forgotten.'

'It is unwise to pay too much, but it is more unwise to pay too little. If you pay too much, you only lose a little money. If you pay too little then you run the risk of losing everything.'

'It is better to have loved a short girl than never to have loved at all' (I just put this in to see if anyone actually reads it!)

194

Practical Tip No 76

Gestures

This would normally be used after a discount has been requested. When people say 'is that your best price?' or 'could you do any better than that?'

The response is, 'Anything else would just be a gesture.'

In reality you are saying the price is close to the limit. The effect is that some people change the subject from discounting to something like delivery. Others will ask how much of a gesture could you give? Either way, you have made a sale without giving too much away.

I first came across this strategy in a jeweller's shop. The owner used it as a first line strategy when I asked for a discount. I got £5 off a ring costing many hundreds of pounds. And I thought I was good at negotiation!

One of my clients was very taken by this tip. The day after I taught it, he took a telephone call from a client.

The client said, 'This quotation, Tom, is that the best price you can do?'

Tom responded, 'Bill, anything else would just be a gesture.'

Bill, 'When can you deliver?'

Tom was amazed! His normal response would have been, 'Can you leave it with me and I will see what I can do?'

Practical Tip No 77

Decision Making

Whether we are buying for profit or knowing we are going to make a loss, affects the decisions we make.

First of all, I need to explain. Why would anyone buy something knowing they are going to lose?

A showroom opens up selling cookers. They buy a cooker for £300. How much is the cooker worth to them? They are buying, expecting a gain. They hope it will attract £6-700.

A customer comes into the showroom. She buys the cooker for £650. The cooker gets delivered and is working well. How much is the cooker worth? Could she get £500 for it? In one year, it may only be worth half of what she paid for it.

When you buy a car you lose more than 15% driving it out of the forecourt. Generally, end users are buying something knowing they will make a loss.

This affects our decision-making.

When we buy for a possible gain, we are much more conservative. When we buy knowing there is a certain loss, we are much more speculative.

When a salesperson from a manufacturer sells to a retail business, they are trying to get the owners to be more speculative. They ask them to take in new ranges, have more stock, advertise and so on. The owners will tend to be more cautious and will want to stick with what they know.

With the showroom owner, always emphasise the lack of risk. Refer to other showrooms, trends, success stories and so on.

You should also use comparison theory (tip no 58). Always present a more speculative option first. This gives the perception that other propositions are more conservative.

When customers come into the showroom, they are more speculative. For a little bit extra, they can get a much better model. Always up-sell people who are buying, knowing there will be a loss. It is much easier to do than with people who are buying expecting a gain.

Practical Tip No 78

Four Differentiators

In the absence of any difference between two options, people will choose the lower price. Your job as a salesperson is to show that there is a differentiation between two options and that the differentiation is worth the additional cost.

There are as many theories on *Features* and *Benefits* as there are days in the year. I will explain what I mean by features and benefits. I think all features should be explained and so the *features, advantages and benefits* model seems to fit the bill for me.

My definitions are:

Features

A feature is a fact that very few people would disagree with. A car has four wheels. This car has ABS braking system. This car has airbags for the driver and passengers.

Advantage

This is an explanation of the feature and how it works. Why did the designer put it in the product in the first place.

- The four wheels make the car more stable on the road.
- The ABS braking system eases off the power to wheels that are skidding.
- Airbags inflate in certain serious accidents to prevent you from hitting the steering wheel with your head.

You will by now probably have worked out I am not an expert in cars! I use them as an example because most readers are familiar with cars. (When I was writing this, I was seriously doubting if I could give an accurate description of ABS!)

197

Benefits

I treat benefits as opinions. They are what you think they do for the customer. As opinions, some people can and do disagree. Also I don't think some prospects want to hear your opinion.

When presenting to these prospects, ask them a question about the benefits. Say for example, that ABS braking eases off the power to wheels that are skidding, so how do you think that would help you?

Another technique would be to say why the designers included the feature. For example, the ABS braking system eases off the power to wheels. The designers are trying to make a skid less likely and to give you more control of the car. What the designers were trying to do may not be an opinion.

My opinion of ABS is that it makes it safer for the car users. Some people would disagree with this. I understand that when a car is driving in a straight line on a dry surface, the stopping distance correlates with the amount of rubber left on the road!

Since ABS reduces this, then in certain conditions, ABS is less safe. It depends on your driving. Some modern cars allow for the driver to switch off the ABS.

The benefits of airbags are opinions. The latest airbags are designed to take account of the driving position and weight of the driver. Some injuries (notably broken jaws!) were being caused by the airbags!

I think it is wrong however to assume that everybody buys for benefits. If that were true, why would anyone in Holland by a mountain bike? Why would anyone buy a 14-day timer on a video recorder that they don't know how to programme?

How could you sell a five-band graphic equaliser on a hi-fi when hardly anyone can even explain what it does? And as for calling it a graphic equaliser, what turkey decided this? I don't get any graphics on my hi-fi!! I get sound, not pictures!!

There are some people who are bells and whistles people. They buy this one because it has more features than that one. The opposite is the case as well, of course (see tip no 12 – *The Economic Buyer*)

So, as a salesperson, my tip is to consider features and benefits as three possibilities:

They can be:

- **Standard**
- **Company**
- **Differentiators**

Standard

A standard feature is one that appears on every product in this class. People in general do not decide to buy on the basis of standard features. When selling, I recommend not making a big thing about standard features.

When selling a car for example, I would mention the features that are standard saying 'It has all the features you would expect from a car of this class including (and then list them)'.

If they are standard features, you can't afford (except possibly with Owls, see tip no 39) to give the advantages and benefits of each one. If the customer shops around, and most do, they will get bored very quickly if everyone explained everything.

If you keep your ears open, you will sometimes get the opportunity to mention the advantages and benefits of standard features. You should always offer to explain how they work if the prospect wants to know.

Company

A company feature and benefit is one associated by the company, e.g Ford have been in business for just over 100 years.

Only mention these company features to people who see the glass as half empty (tip no 49)

Differentiators

The real reason people buy your product, or buy it from you is that they see some differentiation. In essence they feel that what you are offering them is something different from what others offer.

Kwik Fit used a technique – they would get your car onto their ramp in order to sell. Their differentiation was often simply that your car was on their ramp.

87 Practical Tips for Dynamic Selling

Let's say your car needs a new exhaust. You phone garage A and they tell you the cost for a front box is £180, if you need only the back box it costs £160. If you need a complete system it costs £320. You phone the next garage and they say roughly the same, perhaps a little more expensive, perhaps a little less.

Then you phone Kwik Fit.

Their salesperson says, 'There are different types of exhausts for your model and we don't want to give you wrong advice over the phone. In addition, it is unlikely you would need a complete exhaust anyway. Why don't you bring the car down, I will get my mechanic Brian to put it up on a ramp and then we can check exactly what it needs?'

They would then go on to use an alternative close (see tip no 81 – *Closing*) on the time for a suitable appointment.

The people at Kwik Fit know that when you come down and they get your car on their ramp they increase their chances of a sale. They will show you the big hole in the exhaust.

Then they say, 'Unfortunately, you do need a complete exhaust. They aren't normally a stock item but luckily we just happen to have one in stock. It is actually one that was ordered for a customer who was supposed to come in two days ago but he didn't turn up. I can fit it right now for you.'

The chances are this sale is no longer price sensitive, it is about convenience and you will even pay a little more. If they had quoted you on the telephone then they would only have got the job based on low price. Their differentiation is not about the exhaust – it is about getting your car on their ramp.

The confusing part is that a differentiator could be a standard or a company Feature. For example, Volvo chose to make safety their differentiation. The thing I remember about Volvo ads was SIPS (Side Impact Protection System). Was that a differentiator? No, absolutely not. On almost every car in that class, there was a side impact protection system. Were they the first? I am told it was Saab that invented a Side Impact Protection System.

How was it a differentiator then?

A differentiator is something you major on, that other people are

200

87 Practical Tips for Dynamic Selling

ignoring. Volvo chose safety because everyone else was focussing on something else. Apparently, only 7% of car ads mention safety.

Others' ignoring something is as critical as your majoring on it to create a differentiator.

If there is a case for 'mystery shopping' for me, it is the salespeople that should mystery shop competitors to find out what their competitors are saying to prospects so they can create differentiation.

Of course, some products do have real differentiation. That makes it a little easier. In most markets however, the difference between products is becoming less. Sometimes, when running a course, delegates will tell me there is no difference between their products and their competitors. They will claim they are selling exactly the same product and even the same brand as their competitor.

I believe this ignores the 'soft' side of the product. There is always a difference between your and competitive products. One of the differences is you! You sell your own products – you don't sell your competitors' products.

We know that the salesperson is a major factor in sales. Your results are directly related to your ability. Of course there are other things that are differentiators such as the location, stock availability, service levels, after sales care and so on, but the major factor that drives your sales is you.

Even your product knowledge is a differentiator. People will pay more to someone with greater product knowledge. That is why specialist camera shops exist. They may be more expensive but the staff are more knowledgeable than their high street competitors. Not everyone perhaps, but that is more to do with marketing and selling skills than choice.

If you feel that what you sell is exactly the same as others, then make how you treat prospects and customers your target. Improve your own skills and treat them better and your results will improve.

Given that you now have some differentiation between you and your competitor, you should focus on finding at least four of them.

4 is the magic number. Always mention at least four differentiators in your summary close. (see tip no 81)

Practical Tip No 79

Trust the Customer

If you want to develop trust in someone, you have to trust them first. How many signals do you give your customers that you don't trust them?

When I check into hotels, one of the first signals they give is that they don't trust you. I checked into an hotel where I was staying for 19 days. The client was paying for everything except the mini bar. The receptionist wanted my credit card. I promised I wouldn't use anything in the mini-bar. What do you think the response was?

Hotels are not alone. Have a think about your own company procedures. How many of them tell the customer how little you trust them? I never have a written contract with any of my clients. I do all my business on the basis of trust.

One group I was working with did the exercise on eight contacts (see tip no 40 – *Spare Tyre*). One of their contact reasons was to open an account for the customer just in case they did need anything.

We had quite a discussion on this.

If you are talking about developing new business that is less price sensitive, I can think of no better way than breaking your own rules to help someone in a crisis.

Let's take the scenario. Someone you have been prospecting needs one of your products urgently. I actually had a situation when a prospect was losing over £100,000 per hour because a production line was down.

You should help the person out – whether they have an account or not! Forget getting the forms completed. Worry about getting them out of the crisis and then pick up the pieces later.

Because of reciprocity (tip no 41), you will gain one more customer that is not as price sensitive. The fact that you have broken rules to help them makes them feel even more obliged.

Trust is a wonderful thing. When we develop trust in others,

87 Practical Tips for Dynamic Selling

selling is much easier. Your job is to develop trust in others.

I want to be a little careful here because, in my experience, most sales managers believe I haven't completed that last sentence. They think I should have said, 'Your job is to develop trust in others and then exploit that trust!'

Many organisations, in my opinion, exploit the trust of their customers. I have heard statements such as it is five times (or even ten times) more expensive to get a new customer than to keep an existing one. Most companies make more profit from existing customers than from new customers. In essence, existing customers pay for the failed efforts to attract new customers.

Who provides the profit which allows your organisation to pitch for a piece of business that you lose? It is the existing customers. Why would they want to pay to bring in others and potentially dilute the service they receive?

In my experience, most pitches for big new business are keenly priced. In many industries, you get a better deal from being disloyal than loyal – the credit card company that will give you 0% interest on transferred balances; the mortgage company that will give you a discounted rate on your first 6 months if you transfer your mortgage; the catalogue company that gives you a money-off voucher on your first purchase.

One company told me they wanted a training course for salespeople to increase the loyalty of their customers. They wanted me to give them renewal and negotiation techniques that could keep their customers for another year. I asked them why this was an objective. Answer, because they make more profit from existing customers than new ones.

For me, this means the company should stop making so much money and provide a more attractive deal for existing customers. I am not saying they should reduce prices here, although I wouldn't exclude loyalty discounts, I am saying a better deal.

For example, they were a good company but the salespeople, as salespeople do, had a tendency towards talking up the quality of their service when selling. Not in a major way but I don't think you would expect a salesperson to do otherwise. Very few salespeople will point

87 Practical Tips for Dynamic Selling

out how often they deliver late!.

When I spoke with the salespeople, they told me the major problem at renewal was that the service this company provided just wasn't up to scratch. When they entered into a renewal they felt under such pressure because of the complaints of poor service they were lucky to get renewal on any basis!

Businesses should also focus on making the same profit from new customers as they do from existing ones. I understand the need to spread the cost of acquisition over the average life expectancy of a customer, but there is no way existing customers should be subsidising new customers.

My recommendation was to give a better deal by spending some of the additional profit they were seeking on improving the service levels. They had a chronic staff shortage and weren't giving the sales team a fighting chance.

I have always been happier selling a genuinely superior product. I really don't care if it is more expensive and I don't care how much more expensive. I have sold products that were 12 times more expensive than our nearest competitor with great success. The salespeople I feel sorry for are the ones that know their product or service is substandard.

In the absence of evidence, you must believe the customer, for example, when a customer has a complaint. If you have no evidence, you must believe the customer. You cannot expect customers to trust you if you don't trust them.

If you want to develop trust in someone, you have to trust them first.

Practical Tip No 80

When to Close

A lot of salespeople have difficulty learning when and how to close and the easy answer is you should try closing too hard, too early and too often. In this way you will get feedback from the prospect which you can learn from.

Lets face it, people will rarely say to you, 'You could have closed me five minutes ago – I was ready to buy then.' Or 'You were too nice asking me to buy then – I would have preferred you to be a bit more persistent.'

You will always get feedback if you do it too hard, too early and too often. Eventually you will learn!

I always watch for language change when I am selling. The language changes when prospects have *mentally* bought your product or service.

For example, when I am selling a training course, the prospect may say, 'If we did go ahead with you, what would you include?'

Later, the language changes and the 'if' is dropped, e.g. 'What departments could be included in the training?'

Later still, 'Now, do you want us to include experienced and new salespeople on the same course?'

Then I will get, 'We also need you to cover training for the scenario where people ask for a discount at the end.'

They have obviously mentally bought. I can close on the timing of the training. I don't need to ask the if they are going ahead. This is a great use of the Assumptive close. (See next tip)

Practical Tip No 81

Closing Techniques

The best salespeople don't use many different closing techniques - they get the customer so excited by their proposition that the customer closes them. Great salespeople have customers saying, 'How quickly can you deliver?'

The close for great salespeople becomes a natural flowing part of showing what comes next.

Just in case you are not a great salesperson, here are a few of the techniques that I was taught. Sometimes it is helpful to avoid using a direct close as some customers find it hard to make a decision.

Summary

The summary close is the most effective method of closing and so I think it should be used every time.

In tip no 78 – *Four Differentiators*, I said that you need to have just four differentiators to make virtually certain of a sale.

The summary close means you summarise the four differentiators and then ask for the business.

Example – 'So you are getting the model with the 5mm thicker metal which will last longer. The four-year guarantee to protect you and it has the four settings so you can tackle a variety of jobs. It also comes in the colour you were looking for, shall we go ahead with the order?'

Summarise the benefits, ask for the order and STFU! (tip no 68 – *Objections*)

Direct

A direct close is a direct closed question, e.g. 'Do you want to go ahead?'

Open
Good for Owls and Doves (see tip no 39 – *Behaviour*). This is an open question about future action, e.g. 'How do feel about moving to the next stage?'

Alternative
This offers the option between two positive outcomes rather than deciding yes or no, e.g. 'Do you want it in red or blue?'

Assumptive
This is also a good close for Doves. You assume you are getting the business and don't actually ask them – you just go ahead with ordering for them and then they have to stop you.

Minor issue
Usually used as or in conjunction with an assumptive close. This is where you ask a question about something insignificant. When they answer this question, it is clear they are going ahead, e.g. 'We only deliver to your area on Wednesday – is this coming Wednesday okay for you?'

The important thing about the assumptive and the minor issue closes is that you must never ask them if they are going ahead. For example, I was coaching a salesman who used a minor issue close. He said, 'What is the address for delivery?' The customer told him the address and he responded, 'So you want to go ahead then?' Sorry ... wrong!

Prescription (also called the Duke of Wellington or Winston Churchill)
This has to be the worst close I have ever been taught and if any salesperson tried this on me they would be sent on their merry way with a small insect in their listening apparatus!

The prescription close is where you help someone by saying, 'You know, when Churchill had a decision to make, he would list all the pros and cons on a piece of paper.'

Then you would help the prospect to list all the pros for buying the

87 Practical Tips for Dynamic Selling

product.

When it comes to considering the cons over buying, you leave them for a few minutes thinking about the cons. When they have difficulty you help them by adding 'the price' to the cons.

At the end you are supposed to have a long list of pros and a small list of cons. If you are selling to me you are more likely to feel cold (being back in the great outdoors – outside my place of business!!)

I am sure many people use this very successfully.

Practical Tip No 82

Getting Your Next Appointment

One thing you should always do when closing is to ask for the next appointment.

If you make appointments when selling, you probably spend an enormous amount of time on the telephone. You may find that most of that time is spent talking to voice mail, secretaries, colleagues etc.

The connect-through rate I think has dropped dramatically recently. The connect-through rate is the number of times you actually get to speak with the person you are calling.

When you have an appointment and you are at a meeting, ask for your next appointment now. It is far easier to cancel or rearrange an appointment than it is to organise one in the first place. This also fills up your diary well in advance, making use of the scarcity principle (scarce things seem to be more attractive).

In telephone selling, you can ask for an 'appointment' by asking the best time to contact and preferred methods of contact.

Practical Tip No 83

Create an Objection

There are some customers who manage to skilfully combine not objecting with not buying. For example, they say everything is fine and they want to buy and they need the approval of someone else. Some people say they want to buy and they will buy next week. There is no objection about buying, they will buy, but not now.

There was a study conducted in the 1980s which found that in only 37% of sales calls, was an objection ever voiced.

When an objection was expressed, on 64% of the occasions, the salesperson went on to successfully handle the objection and get a sale. Only 21% of the time did the salesperson fail to get a sale.

In these cases, my tip is to **create an objection**.

You can do this by saying:

'In my experience, there are only three reasons people don't buy from me.'

You need to pause here and wait for some indication that you should carry on.

'The first is if they don't like me! And I understand that, I wouldn't buy from someone I don't like!'

You need to wait here until the prospect confirms that it is not you!

'The second reason is that they don't like the product and I can understand that – I wouldn't buy something I didn't like.'

You may have to ask a question here to get them to commit to the product being suitable for them.

'Then that only leaves the third reason. That is the price – it is a little too expensive, isn't it?'

If you decide to use this, then I will go through this carefully because if you don't use it in exactly the way that I have described it will fail.

You must go through the reasons one by one and get confirmation at each stage. This is because you are not telling the truth – there are

87 Practical Tips for Dynamic Selling

much more than three reasons people don't buy! I know I may offend some people here who may say this is unethical.

I am not making any moral judgements here. Don't shoot the newsreader. I am describing the technique, not advocating its use. Anyone can buy my book. If a buyer wants to buy to spot the techniques being used, please feel free.

I have recommended reading Cialdini's book (tip no 28) which was written for the express purpose of highlighting such things to buyers.

The value of using the technique is to close escape routes. Selling has been likened to leading a prospect down a corridor. All the way down the corridor there are open escape doors. Your job is to close each door as you approach it and lead the prospect to the sale at the end. When you use the technique the way I have described, you are closing the escape routes.

Three reasons

If you say to a prospect, 'You know there are only three reasons people don't buy from me – it is either me, the product or the price, which is it?', you will fail.

When you say, 'In my experience, there are only three reasons people don't buy from me,' pausing for an answer means that, when you move on, the prospect has implicitly accepted that there are only three reasons.

'The first is if they don't like me! And I understand that – I wouldn't buy from someone I don't like!'

People never say it is because they don't like you. Not to me anyway!

'The second reason is if they don't like the product and I can understand that – I would buy something I didn't like.'

People usually say the product is great. If not, then you have your objection and you have achieved your objective which was to create an objection. You should now move on to handling the real objection (see tip no 68).

'Then that only leaves the third reason. That is the price, it is a little too expensive isn't it.'

87 Practical Tips for Dynamic Selling

You are using a positive followed by a negative to get a positive answer (see tip no 33)

When you have an agreement that the price is the problem, you would move to handling a price objection. Do not immediately look at price negotiation.

Practical Tip No 83a

Savers

This isn't really a tip for salespeople and so doesn't count in the 86!

I don't know why it is that people get on their high horse about moral standards in selling. I think you see examples of bad ethics day in day out in many industries. I even see examples of bad ethics in the financial world from some of our most prestigious organisations. Not the Swiss private banks I train, I hasten to add.

A few years ago, the Government pointed out unethical practice from banks and building societies. They threatened to legislate unless the financial institutions stopped making account types obsolete.

What happened was that you put your money into a 'Special Saver' account. The banks and building societies made the account obsolete (reducing the interest of course). They replaced it with a 'Special Saver Plus' account.

Most people didn't notice that the interest rate had dropped and there are millions of pounds still left in these 'obsolete' accounts with a peppercorn interest.

Obviously, given the threat of the Government action, the financial institutions stopped the practice immediately.

So now when you put your money in the 'Special Saver Plus' account and leave it there, it becomes a non-preferred account. The preferred account is a 'Special Saver Plus 50' account. Oh, did I forget to mention that non-preferred accounts get a lower rate of interest.

It also gives the financial institutions an opportunity to show how well they look after you. If you go into a branch, the nice sales assistant will tell you there is a better place for your money. The millions of people who never go into a branch just get a lower rate of interest.

Here is my tip for savers.

Never keep your money in the same account for more than 12 months! Become a 'rate tart' and move your money around from building society to bank and back again.

Practical Tip No 84

Complaints

Gathered from a number of sources I have examined, these facts give a lot of food for thought.

- Service companies can lose between 10% and 18% of their customers annually.
- Increasing customer retention by as little as 5% can raise profits by 25% to 30%.
- A customer will tell ten people about a bad service experience and five about a good one.
- At any one time, up to one in four of your customers are likely to be unhappy enough to stop doing business with you.
- Of these, only 4% will complain to senior management.
- In companies that share customer evaluations with service providers and support staff, customer satisfaction ratings jump from 50% to 81% in comparison with those that do not.
- Customer satisfaction ratings double when organisations set standards for responding to customer complaints or questions, and set standards to minimise waiting time for customers.
- Cutting defection rates to 5% can increase net value for each customer by 75%.
- Organisations with concise, understandable and actionable service strategies and a vision are four times as likely to receive superior service ratings from their customers as those without them.
- In organisations where employees understand their roles in the service delivery process, customer satisfaction rates are double those in organisations where customer-focused roles and activities have not been defined (76% versus 35%).
- Every 2% improvement in the rating of your quality by customers is associated with a 1% increase in return on investment.

87 Practical Tips for Dynamic Selling

Let me give you a few tips for handling complaints. Normally, when people complain, the behaviour that causes problems is 'Eagle' behaviour (see tip no 39 – *Behaviours*). My first tip is to follow the guidelines for Eagles:

1. Ask a future opinion question such as, 'I am really sorry that has happened/you are feeling that way. I would like to sort it out for you as quickly as possible. What do I need to do to sort it out for you?' (I am deliberately using the personal pronoun here.)
2. Don't interrupt.
3. Don't use the words 'think', 'basically' or 'obviously'.
4. Don't give your opinion.
5. Don't get in an argument about what you can't do. Say, 'I can't do that – what I can do is ...'
6. Take personal responsibility and sort it out.
7. Deal with it yourself.
8. Discover just how powerful the word 'sorry' is when it is meant.

When a customer complains

20% just want an apology and a quick solution.
30% want less than you are prepared to give them.
30% want the same as you are prepared to give them.
20% want more than you are prepared to give them.

The only people that cause a problem are the 20% that want more than you are prepared to give. Asking people what they want you to do doesn't change the percentages. It only identifies the people you may have a problem with.

When someone is asking for too much, I tackle it two ways. The first makes use of human psychology that says if I ask you the same question twice you will give me a different answer the second time. Children are a very good example of this.

I asked my young daughter, 'What is the capital of France?' She said 'F!'. I asked again, 'What is the capital of France?' She said 'Paris'. A third time, 'What is the capital of France?' She said, 'I don't know, is it Rome?'

If someone asks for too much, my first strategy is to look the individual straight in the face and say, 'What would you really want (or expect) me to do?'

If that strategy doesn't work, then focus on what you can do. Don't get into an argument about what you can't do. Say, 'I can't do that, what I can do is ...'

Who deals with complaints?

When the first person who hears the complaint handles it, 77% of complainants are satisfied or very satisfied with the outcome.

If the first person in your organisation that hears the complaint passes the problem to another person or department, only 61% are happy with the outcome.

The percentage drops steadily until, if it isn't dealt with until the 6th person, only 4% are satisfied. Usually that is now at head office level.

When it gets to the 6th person, guess what? They still have to find a solution. All complaints have to be resolved eventually. In order to resolve it, the 6th person usually has to give them what they were asking for in the first place! Sometimes they have to give more.

I have personal experience of this at the moment. I bought a fitted office from Neville Johnson of Manchester. Name and shame I say! My wife and I were delighted with the products and the installation. There was a tiny problem and, because the first person who heard the complaint became very defensive, it has escalated to the point where I want to name and shame them.

We are now at the third person and I am certain it will go further. The main problem is that they will insist in promising that they will phone back and don't. They also want to prevent me from speaking to anyone senior. It is their reluctance that will drive me to do so in the very near future.

I also think in many companies that the decision not to resolve a complaint at the first level is often done for emotional rather than commercial reasons. The first person that hears the complaint takes it personally. Because of this, my tip is to have a rule that the first person can say 'yes' to a complainant but they cannot say 'no'.

If someone is going to say 'no', it should be a manager. This also

87 *Practical Tips for Dynamic Selling*

has the added value that it takes advantage of our reluctance to bring bad news.

Let me explain our reluctance to be the bearer of bad news. I will relate the content of an experiment.

> In the experiment, someone was left alone in a room and the telephone rang. When the person answered the telephone, they were asked, 'Can you ask Bill in the next room to come to the telephone. I have some bad news for him'. Almost everyone will walk up to Bill and say, 'Bill, there is a telephone call for you'.
>
> Under the same conditions, if the request is, 'Can you ask Bill to come to the telephone – I have some good news for him', almost everyone will walk up to Bill and say, 'Bill, come quickly – there is some good news for you.'

The impact of this in complaints is that I noticed bosses are much happier telling the salesperson to go to the customer and say 'no' than they are doing it themselves.

I am sure you have seen the situation. The boss says 'no we won't do that'. The salesperson communicates the answer, the customer goes ballistic. They want to speak to the boss (dropping satisfaction levels). The boss, when confronted with the customer, agrees to do what they told you they wouldn't do. We don't like to be the bearer of bad news.

All complaints should be dealt with, bearing in mind commercial reality. Emotional considerations of who is right and who is wrong shouldn't be allowed to cloud the issue.

I recently worked with a client that had just resolved a long running complaint. A new branch manager had taken over and they decided they would go to see the customer. After listening to the complaint, they decided to solve it by making a $200 payment to the customer.

The customer was happy and said that was all he was asking for all along. They had resolved the complaint. They did a calculation on the customer's account to see how much business they had lost before resolving the complaint. They estimated $80,000!!

You may be right but if you lose, don't lose the lesson!

Practical Tip No 85

Dormant Accounts

I listened to a salesperson call a dormant account and say something like, 'I noticed you haven't bought anything for the past six months. Is there anything you need?'

They are really saying, 'I am so inefficient I didn't notice for six months!'

What are they expecting the customer to say? 'Thank goodness you called, I have been lost without you. Alternative suppliers are difficult to find and are rubbish! I may even have had to close my business because of a lack of alternatives!'

It isn't going to happen. People stop buying from you for a reason. When following up a dormant account, assume there was a problem. Calling to say something like, 'Hi, I think we may have upset you and I was calling to see if I could try to sort it out', is a better approach. At least you have the chance of finding out what went wrong.

Occasionally, you will get the reply that the person has been away, retired or whatever. The 'assuming something is wrong' approach doesn't lose anything in these circumstances. The other approach always loses.

Practical Tip No 86

Use Your Results to Be the Best

To be successful, you need to measure your results. By results I mean *activity v success*.

- How many people do you have to approach in order to engage a prospect? On the telephone, this would be called your connect-through rate. Face to face, it is when you engage in a conversation about your products or their needs.
- How many do you have to engage with in order to get to a presentation of your products?
- How many do you give information in the form of a presentation to compared with how often you get to a proposal stage?
- How often do you get to a proposal stage compared with how many orders you get?
- If you get an order, what is your average order value?
- If you get an order, how many product lines does it have?

In one company I worked for, we increased our sales by drawing a red line on an order form. In our company, an average order had three product lines on it. It was unusual to get an order with more than six product lines. We drew a red line under the space for the 6th product. Somehow, mentally it caused salespeople to get more product lines. We thought they were trying to get to the red line!

- How many orders do you get compared with how many cancellations you suffer?
- How many repeat orders do you get?

These measurements tell you where to improve. For example, if you need to get in touch with ten people to engage one, then you need some attention grabbing strategies.

Practical Tip No 86

If out of ten people you engage, only one gets involved in a presentation, you need help statements that build the need.

If out of ten presentations you only get to one proposal, you need to handle more objections within your presentations.

and so on.....

These figures vary depending on the industry and business. For example, a double glazing company needs to contact more people before engaging one than a travel agent.

Whatever level of performance you produce you will discover where to improve by looking at your activity.

Most organisations record and measure historical data. That is like the captain of the Titanic asking, 'What was that we just hit?' If you measure activity, you should know what your activity will produce based on your closing ratios.

What gets measured gets done!

Be The Best!

If you wanted to bet on the winner of a golf tournament, who would you bet on?

- The longest driver? — If so bet on John Daly (Tiger Woods is ranked 7th)

- The most accurate driver? — Bet on Joe Durant (Tiger Woods is 96th)

- The player who hits most greens in regulation? — Tom Lehman (Tiger Woods is 5th)

- Least putts per round? — Craig Kanada (Tiger Woods is 87th)

- Most Eagles — Brad Faxon (Tiger Woods is 21st)

- Most Birdies — Phil Mickelson (Tiger Woods is 55th)

- Best percentage of saves from sand — Franklin Langham (Tiger Woods is 154th)

- **Or the highest world ranked Player?** — **Tiger Woods is Number 1!**

Go for all round improvement for the highest rewards.

If Bill Glasson had managed a 4% improvement in his golf (average strokes 71.09 to 68.43 per round), he may have achieved Tiger Woods' winnings of $6.6 million instead of the $840,000 he did win.

Most people are not competing at the very top level and the figures get more incredible the further down you go.

For example, if Curtis Strange could have improved his performance by less than 1% (from 71.57 to 71.02), he may have won the $1.5 million Ted Tryba won instead of the $118,000 he won.

Source **pgatour.com** tour stats for 2001

Go for the BBBOP method – Be Better By One Percent.

**You don't have to be the best –
you just have to be the best you can be.**

Thank you for reading the book. If you have implemented any of the tips, I am sure your sales will have improved as a result.

I do love to hear stories of what happens. Please feel free to email me at **david@gtiuk.com** with any stories, tips, suggestions, comments and other bits of information or gossip that I can put into my next book.